A Text book on Laplace Transform

by

Dr. Brijesh Kumar Tripathi and Dr. V. K. Chaubey

I dedicate this work to our beloved family....

Brijesh Kumar Tripathi and V. K. Chaubey

Preface

The study of mathematical transformations has significantly contributed to the progress of science and engineering, with the Laplace Transform being a key tool. Named after the French mathematician Pierre-Simon Laplace, this powerful method provides a connection between time-domain and frequency domain representations of functions, making complex mathematical problems, especially those involving differential equations, much easier to solve.

The Laplace Transform is an essential tool for modeling dynamic systems, solving linear ordinary differential equations (ODEs), and analyzing system stability and behavior in fields like control theory, signal processing, and systems analysis. By converting time-dependent functions into an algebraic form, it transforms challenging differential equations into simpler algebraic equations, making them easier to solve and comprehend. Additionally, the Inverse Laplace Transform allows for a return to the time-domain solution, making it a comprehensive tool for analyzing real-world problems in engineering, physics, economics, and more. In this exploration, we will cover the Laplace Transform, including its definition, key properties, applications, and techniques for calculating both Laplace and Inverse Laplace Transforms and its applications in the area control theory, Electrical Engineering, Mechanical systems, signal processing and other areas, providing both theoretical understanding and practical tools for its implementation. Whether you're a student studying foundational concepts or a professional looking to deepen your understanding of system dynamics, the Laplace Transform offers valuable insights into the behavior and solutions of complex systems.

Brijesh Kumar Tripathi and V. K. Chaubey

Introduction

Integral transformations have played a pivotal role in solving problems in applied mathematics, mathematical physics, and engineering sciences for over two centuries. The development of these transformations, including the Laplace and Fourier transforms, stems from the groundbreaking contributions of Pierre-Simon Laplace (1749–1827) and Joseph Fourier (1768–1830).

In mathematics, an integral transform is an operator that maps a function from its original function space to a different one via the process of integration. This transformation often simplifies the analysis of the function, as certain properties become more evident and easier to handle in the transformed space. The original function can usually be recovered by applying the corresponding inverse transform. Symbolically, an integral transform generates a new function $F(x)$ by integrating the product of a given function $f(t)$ and a kernel function $K(t, x)$ over appropriate limits (a, b). This is represented as:

$$F(x) = \int_a^b K(t, x) f(t) dt \tag{1}$$

FDepending on the choice of the kernel function $K(t, x)$ and the specific limits of integration, the integral transform in equation (1) can be classified into the following types:

1. When $K(t, x) = e^{-st}$, a real-valued function, and the limits of integration are from 0 to ∞, equation (1) becomes:

$$F(x) = \int_0^\infty e^{-st} f(t) dt \tag{2}$$

This transformation is known as the Laplace transform. Initially introduced by the French mathematician Pierre-Simon Laplace, it was later systematically developed by the British physicist Oliver Heaviside (1850–1925) to simplify the solution of differential equations that describe physical processes. Today, the Laplace transform is widely used by electrical engineers to solve ordinary differential equations in electronic circuit and system analysis. It effectively transforms a real-valued function into a new function by multiplying it by e^{-st}, making complex problems easier to handle.

2. When $K(t,x) = e^{ist}$, a complex-valued function, and the limits of integration are from $-\infty$ to ∞, equation (1) becomes:

$$F(x) = \int_{-\infty}^{\infty} e^{ist} f(t)dt \tag{3}$$

This transformation is known as the Fourier transform. Invented by Joseph Fourier, it is a crucial tool in engineering and physics for solving partial differential equations. The Fourier transform has widespread applications in fields such as quantum mechanics, wave motion, the heat equation, Laplace's equation, and turbulence. It converts a function into its frequency-domain representation by mapping it through the complex exponential function e^{ist}, facilitating the analysis and simplification of problems involving periodic or oscillatory phenomena.

3. When $K(t,x) = \frac{2t}{\sqrt{t^2-u^2}}$ and the limits of integration are from u to ∞, equation (1) becomes:

$$F(x) = \int_{u}^{\infty} \frac{2t}{\sqrt{t^2-u^2}} f(t)dt \tag{4}$$

This transformation is known as the Abel transform. Invented by Niels Henrik Abel, it is especially useful in the analysis of spherically symmetric or axially symmetric functions. The Abel transform simplifies complex problems in areas such as astrophysics, potential theory, and wave mechanics by utilizing the inherent symmetries of these functions. It provides a mathematical framework for mapping a function to its integral representation along specific symmetric axes, making it easier to study these systems.

4. When $K(t,x) = t^{u-1}$ and the limits of integration are from 0 to ∞, equation (1) becomes:

$$F(x) = \int_0^\infty t^{u-1} f(t)dt \tag{5}$$

This transformation is known as the Mellin transform. Invented by the Finnish mathematician Hjalmar Mellin, the Mellin transform is an integral transform that can be seen as a multiplicative analogue of the two-sided Laplace transform. It is closely linked to the theory of Dirichlet series and has important applications in number theory, mathematical statistics, and the study of asymptotic expansions. The Mellin transform is related to the Laplace and Fourier transforms, as well as the gamma function and other special functions. Its versatility makes it a valuable tool for solving problems in various branches of mathematics and applied sciences.

5. When $K(t,x) = tJ_v(ut)$, where $J_v(ut)$ represents the Bessel function of the first kind, and the limits of integration are from 0 to ∞, equation (1) becomes:

$$F(x) = \int_0^\infty tJ_v(ut) f(t)dt \tag{6}$$

This transformation is known as the Hankel transformation or Fourier–Bessel transform. First developed by the mathematician Hermann Hankel, this transformation is related to the Fourier–Bessel series over a finite interval, much like the Fourier transform over an infinite interval is connected to the Fourier series over a finite interval.

In addition to the transformations mentioned above, there are numerous other integral transformations linked to various special functions, each defined with particular limits. This book focuses on a detailed study of Laplace transforms.

Contents

Chapter 1

Laplace Transform

1.1 Introduction

The Laplace transform was introduced by the French mathematician Pierre-Simon Laplace and later systematically developed by the British physicist Oliver Heaviside (1850–1925) using operational methods to solve electrical engineering problems. However, Heaviside's approach lacked full rigor and was not entirely systematic. This gap was subsequently addressed and refined by mathematicians like Bromwich and Carson, who provided a more rigorous and comprehensive treatment of the Laplace transform.

The Laplace transform is an essential tool for solving linear ordinary and partial differential equations with constant coefficients, especially when appropriate initial and boundary conditions are provided. The method involves finding the general solution to the equation using the Laplace transform, then determining the arbitrary constants by applying the given initial and boundary conditions. This approach simplifies the solution of complex differential equations, making it easier to analyze and solve problems in fields such as physics and engineering.

The Laplace transform, when applied to a single or a system of linear ordinary differential equations, converts the problem into algebraic equations, making the solution process more straightforward. For partial differential equations with two independent variables, the Laplace transform is applied to one variable, turning the equation into an ordinary differential equation in the other variable. This equation can then be solved using standard methods, and the inverse Laplace transform is used to recover the solution to the original partial differential equation. The Laplace transform is particularly effective in solving mathematical models of physical problems, especially when the differential equation's right-hand side includes a driving force that is discontinuous or short-lived, offering an efficient way to tackle such scenarios and find solutions.

Definition 1.1.1. *Let $f(t)$ be a function defined for all positive value of t. Then, the Laplace transform of $f(t)$ is given by*

$$F(s) = \int_0^\infty e^{-st} f(t)dt$$

provided the integral converges.

Thus, we define the Laplace transform of $f(t)$ as

$$L[f(t)] = F(s) = \int_0^\infty e^{-st} f(t)dt$$

where the symbol L represents the Laplace Transform Operator.

Note: 1. There are two types of Laplace transforms. The integral form described earlier is known as the **one-sided** or **unilateral Laplace transform**. On the other hand, when the transform is defined as $L[f(t)] = F(s) = \int_0^\infty e^{-st} f(t)dt$, where s is a complex variable, it is called the **two-sided** or **bilateral Laplace transform** of $f(t)$, provided the integral converges.

In the case of the unilateral transform, where s is a complex number, the Laplace transform is typically defined over a portion of the complex plane. Specifically, if $Lf(t)$ exists for real s, then $Lf(t)$ exists in the half of the complex plane where $Re\ s > a$ (as shown in Figure 1.1). The transform $F(s)$ is an analytic function with the following properties:

i. $\lim_{Re\ s\to\infty} F(s) = 0$ viz. the necessary condition for $F(s)$ to be a transform.

ii. $\lim_{s\to\infty} sF(s) = A$ if the original function has a limit $\lim_{t\to\infty} f(t) = A$.

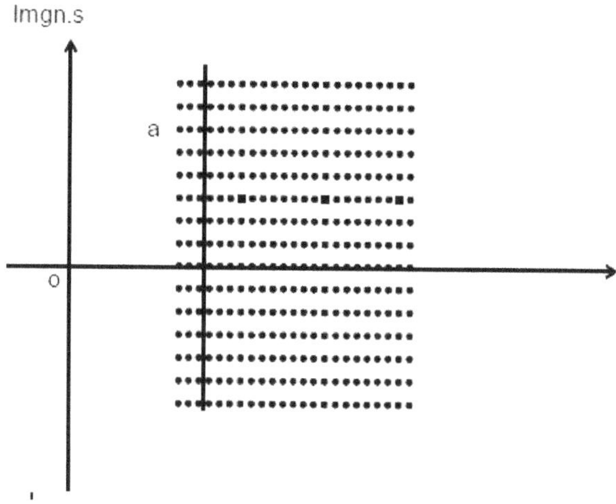

*Fig.*1.1 *Real axis*

2. The Laplace transform does not exist for all functions, but when it does exist, it is uniquely determined. For the Laplace transform to exist, the given function must be continuous on every finite interval and must satisfy the condition of exponential order. Specifically, there must be positive constants M and 'a' such that $|f(t)| \leq Me^{at}$ for all $t \geq 0$. A function $f(t)$ that satisfies this condition is sometimes referred to as the "object function," defined for all $t \geq 0$, and its Laplace transform $F(s)$ is the resulting "image function." In this context, the parameter a should be chosen large enough to ensure the convergence of the integral.

Thus, the condition for the existence of $F(s)$ is sufficient but not necessary, meaning that if the above condition is met, the Laplace transform of $f(t)$ will definitely exist. However, while satisfying this condition increases the likelihood of the Laplace transform existing, it does not guarantee that all such functions will have a Laplace transform, but it is a necessary condition for convergence.

1.2 Laplace Transform of Elementry functions

By direct definition of laplace transform we have following results:

Sr. No.	Elementry Function $f(t)$	Laplace Transform $L[f(t)] = F(s)$
1.	1	$\frac{1}{s}, \quad s > 0$
2.	e^{at}	$\frac{1}{s-a}, \quad s > a$
3.	t^n	$\frac{n!}{s^{(n+1)}}, \quad$ for $n = 0, 1, 2, ...$ otherwise $\frac{\Gamma(n+1)}{s^{(n+1)}}$
4.	$\sin at$	$\frac{a}{s^2+a^2} \quad s > 0$
5.	$\cos at$	$\frac{s}{s^2+a^2} \quad s > 0$
6.	$\sinh at$	$\frac{a}{s^2-a^2} \quad s > \|a\|$
7.	$\cosh at$	$\frac{s}{s^2-a^2} \quad s > \|a\|$

Proof:-1. Since laplace transform of a function $f(t)$ is given by

$$L[f(t)] = F(s) = \int_0^\infty e^{-st} f(t) dt$$

Now subustiting $f(t) = 1$ in above equation we have

$$L[1] = F(s) = \int_0^\infty e^{-st} dt$$

Integrating above equation we have

$$L[1] = F(s) = [-\frac{e^{-st}}{s}]_0^\infty$$

this implies that

$$L[1] = [-\frac{e^{-\infty}}{s} + \frac{e^0}{s}] = -0 + \frac{1}{s} = \frac{1}{s}.$$

2. Since laplace transform of a function $f(t)$ is given by

$$L[f(t)] = F(s) = \int_0^\infty e^{-st} f(t) dt$$

Now subustiting $f(t) = e^{at}$ in above equation we have

$$L[e^{at}] = F(s) = \int_0^\infty e^{at} e^{-st} dt = \int_0^\infty e^{-(s-a)t} dt$$

Integrating above equation we have

$$L[e^{at}] = F(s) = [-\frac{e^{-(s-a)t}}{s-a}]_0^\infty$$

this implies that

$$L[e^{at}] = [-\frac{e^{-\infty}}{s-a} + \frac{e^0}{s-a}] = -0 + \frac{1}{s-a} = \frac{1}{s-a}.$$

3. Since laplace transform of a function $f(t)$ is given by

$$L[f(t)] = F(s) = \int_0^\infty e^{-st} f(t)dt$$

Now subustiting $f(t) = t$ in above equation we have

$$L[t] = F(s) = \int_0^\infty e^{-st} tdt$$

Integrating above equation we get

$$L[t] = [-t\frac{e^{-st}}{s} - \frac{e^{-st}}{s^2}]_0^\infty = \frac{1}{s^2}$$

Again when we take $f(t) = t^2$ then we have

$$L[t^2] = [-t^2\frac{e^{-st}}{s} + 2\int t\frac{e^{-st}}{s}dt]_0^\infty = [-t^2\frac{e^{-st}}{s} - 2t\frac{e^{-st}}{s^2} - 2\frac{e^{-st}}{s^3}]_0^\infty = \frac{2}{s^3} = \frac{2!}{s^3}$$

Similarily we get

$$L[t^3] = \frac{3!}{s^4}$$

In continuation of above process we get

$$L[t^n] = \frac{n!}{s^{n+1}} = \frac{\Gamma(n+1)}{s^{n+1}} \qquad \text{since} \quad n! = \Gamma(n+1)$$

4. Since laplace transform of a function $f(t)$ is given by

$$L[f(t)] = F(s) = \int_0^\infty e^{-st} f(t)dt$$

Now subustiting $f(t) = \sin at$ in above equation we have

$$L[\sin at] = F(s) = \int_0^\infty e^{-st} \sin atdt$$

Integrating above equation we have

$$L[\sin at] = \frac{e^{-st}}{s^2+a^2}[-s\sin at - a\cos at]_0^\infty = \frac{a}{s^2+a^2}$$

5. Since laplace transform of a function $f(t)$ is given by

$$L[f(t)] = F(s) = \int_0^\infty e^{-st} f(t)dt$$

Now subustiting $f(t) = \cos at$ in above equation we have

$$L[\cos at] = F(s) = \int_0^\infty e^{-st} \cos at dt$$

Integrating above equation we have

$$L[\cos at] = \frac{e^{-st}}{s^2+a^2}[-s\cos at - a\sin at]_0^\infty = \frac{s}{s^2+a^2}$$

6. Since laplace transform of a function $f(t)$ is given by

$$L[f(t)] = F(s) = \int_0^\infty e^{-st} f(t)dt$$

Now subustiting $f(t) = \sinh at$ in above equation we have

$$L[\sinh at] = F(s) = \int_0^\infty e^{-st} \sinh at dt = \int_0^\infty e^{-st}(\frac{e^{at}-e^{-at}}{2})dt$$

Integrating above equation we have

$$L[\sinh at] = \frac{1}{2}[\frac{1}{s-a} - \frac{1}{s+a}] = \frac{a}{s^2-a^2}$$

7. Since laplace transform of a function $f(t)$ is given by

$$L[f(t)] = F(s) = \int_0^\infty e^{-st} f(t)dt$$

Now subustiting $f(t) = \cosh at$ in above equation we have

$$L[\cosh at] = F(s) = \int_0^\infty e^{-st} \cosh at dt = \int_0^\infty e^{-st}(\frac{e^{at}+e^{-at}}{2})dt$$

Integrating above equation we have

$$L[\cosh at] = \frac{1}{2}[\frac{1}{s-a} + \frac{1}{s+a}] = \frac{s}{s^2-a^2}$$

1.3 Properties of Laplace Transform

Important properties of laplace transform are given below:

Sr. No.	Name of property	Function f(t)	Laplace Transform $L[f(t)] = F(s)$
1.	Linear	$af(t)+bg(t)$	$aF(s)+bG(s)$,
2.	Change of Scale	$f(at)$	$\frac{1}{a}F(\frac{s}{a})$
3.	First Shifting	$e^{at}f(t)$	$F(s-a)$
4.	Second Shifting	$f(t-a)u(t-a)$	$e^{-as}F(s)$
5.	Derivative	$\frac{d^n}{dt^n}f(t)$	$s^nF(s)-s^{n-1}f(0)-s^{n-2}f^{'}(0)-...$ $-f^{n-1}(0)$
6.	Initial value	$\lim_{t\leftarrow 0}f(t)$	$\lim_{s\leftarrow\infty}sF(s)$
7.	Final value	$\lim_{t\leftarrow\infty}f(t)$	$\lim_{s\leftarrow 0}sF(s)$
8.	Multiplication by t	$t^nf(t)$	$(-1)^n\frac{d^n}{ds^n}F(s)$
9.	Integral of a function	$\int_0^t f(t)dt$	$\frac{F(s)}{s}$
10.	Division by t	$\frac{f(t)}{t}$	$\int_s^\infty F(s)ds$
11.	Convolution theorem	$f(t)*g(t)$	$F(s).G(s)$
12.	Periodic Function	$f(t+T)=f(t)$	$\frac{\int_0^T e^{-st}f(t)dt}{1-e^{-sT}}$

Proof: 1. Let $f(t), g(t)$ be the two arbitrary function and $F(s), G(s)$ be their laplace transform respectively then by defination of laplace transform we have

$$L[af(t)+bg(t)] = \int_0^\infty e^{-st}[af(t)+bg(t)]dt$$

where a, b are any arbitrary constant.

$$L[af(t)+bg(t)] = a\int_0^\infty e^{-st}f(t)dt + b\int_0^\infty e^{-st}g(t)dt$$

Thus we have

$$L[af(t)+bg(t)] = aF(s)+bG(s) \qquad \text{(by defnition of laplace transform)}$$

2. Let laplace transform of the function $f(t)$ be $F(s)$ then

$$L[f(at)] = \int_0^\infty e^{-st}f(at)dt$$

Let $at = u$ then $adt = du$, using this in above equation we have

$$L[f(at)] = \int_0^\infty e^{-su/a}f(u)du/a$$

$$\implies L[f(at)] = \frac{1}{a}\int_0^\infty e^{-\frac{s}{a}u}f(u)du$$

$$\implies L[f(at)] = \frac{1}{a}F(\frac{s}{a})$$

3. Let laplace transform of the function $f(t)$ be $F(s)$ then

$$L[e^{at}f(t)] = \int_0^\infty e^{-st}e^{at}f(t)dt$$

$$\implies L[e^{at}f(t)] = \int_0^\infty e^{-(s-a)t}f(t)dt$$

Now let $s - a = p$

$$\implies L[e^{at}f(t)] = \int_0^\infty e^{-pt}f(t)dt$$

$$\implies L[e^{at}f(t)] = F(s-a) \qquad \text{(by definition of laplace transform)}$$

4. Since unit step function $u(t-a)$ is given by

$$u(t-a) = \begin{cases} 0 & \text{when } t < a \\ 1 & \text{when } t \geq a \end{cases} \tag{1.1}$$

Now let laplace transform of the function $f(t)$ be $F(s)$ then

$$L[f(t-a)u(t-a)] = \int_0^\infty e^{-st}f(t-a)u(t-a)dt$$

Using equation (1.1) in above equation we have

$$L[f(t-a)u(t-a)] = \int_0^a e^{-st}f(t-a).0dt + \int_a^\infty e^{-st}f(t-a).1dt$$

$$= \int_a^\infty e^{-st}f(t-a)dt$$

Now let $t - a - p \implies dt = dp$, using this in above equation we have

$$= \int_0^\infty e^{-s(p+a)}f(p)dp$$

$$= e^{-as}\int_0^\infty e^{-sp}f(p)dp$$

$$\implies L[f(t-a)u(t-a)] = e^{-as}F(s)$$

5. Let laplace transform of the function $f(t)$ be $F(s)$ then

$$L[f'(t)] = \int_0^\infty e^{-st}f'(t)dt$$

Integrating by parts, we get

$$L[f'(t)] = [e^{-st}f(t)]_0^\infty - \int_0^\infty (-se^{-st})f(t)dt$$

$$= -f(0) + s\int_0^\infty e^{-st} f(t)dt$$

$$= -f(0) + sF(s) \qquad \text{by definition of laplace transform}$$

$$\implies L[f'(t)] = sL[f(t)] - f(0) \qquad [since\ \ L[f(t)] = F(s)] \tag{1.2}$$

Note: *Roughly laplace transform of derivative of $f(t)$ corresponds to multiplication of laplace transform of $f(t)$ by s.*

Now replacing $f(t)$ by $f'(t)$ and $f'(t)$ by $f''(t)$ in equation (1.2), we get

$$L[f''(t)] = sL[f'(t)] - f'(0) \tag{1.3}$$

Now putting value of $L[f'(t)]$ from equation (1.2) in equation (1.3), we get

$$L[f''(t)] = s[sL[f(t)] - f(0)] - f'(0)$$

$$\implies L[f''(t)] = s^2L[f(t)] - sf(0) - f'(0)$$

similarily we get

$$L[f'''(t)] = s^3L[f(t)] - s^2f(0) - sf'(0) - f''(0)$$

$$\vdots$$

$$L[f^n(t)] = s^nL[f(t)] - s^{(n-1)}f(0) - s^{(n-2)}f'(0) - s^{(n-3)}f''(0) - ... - f^{(n-1)}(0)$$

Thus we have

$$L[f^n(t)] = s^nF(s) - s^{(n-1)}f(0) - s^{(n-2)}f'(0) - s^{(n-3)}f''(0) - ... - f^{(n-1)}(0)$$

6. Since the laplace transform of the derivative of the function is given by

$$L[f'(t)] = sF(s) - f(0)$$

where $F(s)$ be the laplace transform of the function $f(t)$.

Now by definition of laplace transform the above equation can be written as

$$\int_0^\infty e^{-st} f'(t)dt = sF(s) - f(0)$$

taking limit $s \to \infty$ both side of the above equation we have

$$\lim_{s\to\infty} \int_0^\infty e^{-st} f'(t)dt = \lim_{s\to\infty}[sF(s) - f(0)]$$

$$\implies \lim_{s\to\infty} sF(s) = f(0) + \int_0^\infty (\lim_{s\to\infty} e^{-st}) f'(t)dt$$

$$\implies = f(0) + \int_0^\infty 0.f'(t)dt \qquad [since \ \ \lim_{s\to\infty} e^{-st} = 0]$$

$$\implies = f(0) + 0 = f(0) = \lim_{t\to 0} f(t)$$

Thus we have

$$\lim_{s\to\infty} sF(s) = \lim_{t\to 0} f(t)$$

7. Since the laplace transform of the derivative of the function is given by

$$L[f'(t)] = sF(s) - f(0)$$

where $F(s)$ be the laplace transform of the function $f(t)$.

Now by definition of laplace transform the above equation can be written as

$$\int_0^\infty e^{-st} f'(t)dt = sF(s) - f(0)$$

taking limit $s \to 0$ both side of the above equation we have

$$\lim_{s\to 0} \int_0^\infty e^{-st} f'(t)dt = \lim_{s\to 0}[sF(s) - f(0)]$$

$$\implies \lim_{s\to 0}[sF(s) - f(0)] = \lim_{s\to 0} \int_0^\infty e^{-st}) f'(t)dt$$

$$\implies = \int_0^\infty (\lim_{s\to 0} e^{-st}).f'(t)dt = \int_0^\infty f'(t)dt \qquad [since \ \ \lim_{s\to 0} e^{-st} = 1]$$

$$\implies \lim_{s\to 0} sF(s) - f(0) = [f(t)]_0^\infty = f(\infty) - f(0) = \lim_{t\to\infty} f(t)$$

Thus we have

$$\lim_{s\to 0} sF(s) = \lim_{t\to\infty} f(t)$$

8. Let laplace transform of the function $f(t)$ be $F(s)$ then

$$L[f(t)] = F(s) = \int_0^\infty e^{-st} f(t)dt$$

Differentiating above equation w.r.t. $'s'$ we get

$$\frac{d}{ds}F(s) = \frac{d}{ds}\int_0^\infty e^{-st} f(t)dt$$

$$\implies = \int_0^\infty (\frac{d}{ds}e^{-st}) f(t)dt$$

$$\implies = \int_0^\infty (-te^{-st}) f(t)dt = \int_0^\infty e^{-st}(-tf(t))dt$$

$$\frac{d}{ds}F(s) = -L[tf(t)] \qquad \text{[by definition of laplace transform]}$$

$$\implies L[tf(t)] = -\frac{d}{ds}F(s)$$

Similarily we get

$$L[t^2 f(t)] = \frac{d^2}{ds^2}F(s)$$

$$L[t^3 f(t)] = -\frac{d^3}{ds^3}F(s)$$

.

.

.

$$L[t^n f(t)] = (-1)^n \frac{d^n}{ds^n}F(s)$$

9. Let laplace transform of the function $f(t)$ be $F(s)$. Now again let $\phi(t) = \int_0^t f(t)dt$ and $\phi(0) = 0$ then $\phi'(t) = f(t)$.

Now since we know that

$$L[\phi' t] = sL[\phi(t)] - \phi(0)$$

$$\implies L[\phi' t] = sL[\phi(t)] \qquad \text{since } \phi(0) = 0$$

$$\implies L[\phi(t)] = \frac{1}{s}L[\phi' t]$$

Now putting the value of $\phi(t)$ and $\phi' t$ in above equation we have

$$L[\int_0^t f(t)dt] = \frac{1}{s}F(s)$$

10. Let laplace transform of the function $f(t)$ be $F(s)$. Then

$$L[f(t)] = F(s) = \int_0^\infty e^{-st} f(t)dt$$

Integrating above equation w.r.t. $'s'$ by taking limit from s to ∞ we have

$$\int_s^\infty F(s)ds = \int_s^\infty [\int_0^\infty e^{-st} f(t)dt]ds$$

$$\Longrightarrow = \int_0^\infty f(t)[\int_s^\infty e^{-st} ds]dt$$

$$\Longrightarrow = \int_0^\infty \frac{-f(t)}{t}[e^{-st}]_s^\infty dt = \int_0^\infty \frac{-f(t)}{t}[0 - e^{-st}]dt$$

$$\Longrightarrow \int_s^\infty F(s)ds = \int_0^\infty e^{-st} \frac{f(t)}{t} dt = L[\frac{f(t)}{t}]$$

Thus we have

$$L[\frac{f(t)}{t}] = \int_s^\infty F(s)ds$$

11. The definition of convolution of two function is given by

Definition 1.3.1. *Let $f(t)$ and $g(t)$ be two functions of class 'A', then the convolution of the two functions $f(t)$ and $g(t)$ denoted by $f(t) * g(t)$ and defined as:*

$$f(t) * g(t) = \int_0^t f(u)g(t-u)du \tag{1.4}$$

the convolution of two function $f(t) * g(t)$ is also known as falting of $f(t)$ and $g(t)$.

Note: *The convolution of two function always satisfies commutative law, associative law and distributive law over addition.* **Convolution theorem of Laplace transform**

Theorem 1.3.1. *Laplace transform of the convolution of two function is equal to product of laplace transform of both the function. i.e.*

$$L[f(t) * g(t)] = L[f(t)].L[g(t)] = F(s).G(s)$$

where $F(s)$ and $G(s)$ are the laplace transform of the function $f(t)$ and $g(t)$ respectively.

Proof: Let laplace transform of the function $f(t)$ be $F(s)$. Then

$$L[f(t)] = F(s) = \int_0^\infty e^{-st} f(t)dt$$

Then the laplace transform of convolution of two function $f(t) * g(t)$ is given by

$$L[f(t) * g(t)] = \int_0^\infty e^{-st}[f(t) * g(t)]dt$$

Now using equation (1.4) in above equation we get

$$L[f(t) * g(t)] = \int_0^\infty e^{-st}[\int_0^t f(u)g(t-u)du]dt$$

Above expression clearly shows that the integration is I^{st} taken along the vertical strip PQ from $P$to Q, P resting on the curve $u = 0$ and Q resting on the curve $u = t$ and finally the strip PQ slides between $t = 0$ to ∞ to cover the full dotted region.

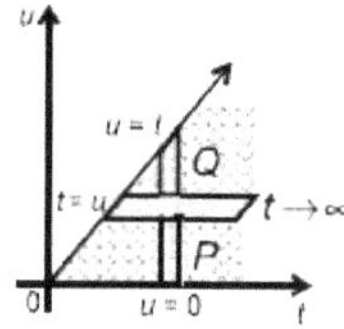

Now on changing the order of integration we have

$$L[f(t) * g(t)] = \int_0^\infty \int_u^\infty e^{-st} f(u)g(t-u)dtdu$$

$$= \int_0^\infty f(u)[\int_u^\infty e^{-st} g(t-u)dt]du$$

Now let $t - u = p \implies dt = dp$, using this in above equation we have

$$L[f(t) * g(t)] = \int_0^\infty f(u)[\int_0^\infty e^{-s(p+u)} g(p)dp]du$$

$$= \int_0^\infty f(u)e^{-su}[\int_0^\infty e^{-sp} g(p)dp]du$$

$$= \int_0^\infty e^{-su} f(u)du.G(s) \qquad \text{[by definition of laplace transform]}$$

$$L[f(t) * g(t)] = F(s).G(s) \qquad \text{[by definition of laplace transform]}$$

Thus we have

$$L[f(t) * g(t)] = F(s).G(s)$$

12. Let $f(t)$ be a periodic function with period T i.e. $f(t+T)=f(t)$. So by definition of laplace transform we have

$$L[f(t)] = \int_0^\infty e^{-st} f(t)dt$$

$$= \int_0^T e^{-st} f(t)dt + \int_T^{2T} e^{-st} f(t)dt + \int_{2T}^{3T} e^{-st} f(t)dt + ...$$

Putting $t=u$, $t=u+T$, $t=u+2T$,........ in successive integrals, we have

$$L[f(t)] = \int_0^T e^{-su} f(u)du + \int_0^T e^{-s(u+T)} f(u+T)du + \int_0^T e^{-s(u+2T)} f(u+2T)du + ...$$

Since $f(u) = f(u+T) = f(u+2T) = ...$, so we have

$$L[f(t)] = \int_0^T e^{-su} f(u)du + e^{-sT}\int_0^T e^{-su} f(u)du + e^{-2sT}\int_0^T e^{-su} f(u)du + ...$$

$$\implies L[f(t)] = (1 + e^{-sT} + e^{-2sT} + e^{-3sT} + ...)\int_0^T e^{-su} f(u)du$$

$$\implies L[f(t)] = \frac{1}{1-e^{-sT}}\int_0^T e^{-su} f(u)du$$

Thus we have

$$L[f(t)] = \frac{1}{1-e^{-sT}}\int_0^T e^{-st} f(t)dt$$

1.4 Solved Problems

Example 1 Find laplace transform of
(i) $\sin 2t \cos 3t$ (ii) $\sin^3 2t$ (iii) $7e^{2t} + 5\cos t + 7t^3 + 2$

(iv) $(\sqrt{t}+\frac{1}{\sqrt{t}})^3$ (v) $e^t t^{-\frac{1}{2}}$ (vi) $f(t) = \begin{cases} \cos t, & \text{when } 0 < t < \pi \\ 0 & \text{when } t > \pi \end{cases}$

(vii) $f(t) = \begin{cases} 1, & 0 \le t < 1 \\ t & 1 \le t < 2 \\ t^2 & 2 \le t < \infty \end{cases}$ (viii) $f(t) = \begin{cases} \sin(t-\frac{\pi}{3}), & t > \frac{\pi}{3} \\ 0 & t < \frac{\pi}{3} \end{cases}$

Sol.: (i) Since $\sin 2t \cos 3t = \frac{1}{2}(2\cos 3t \sin 2t) = \frac{1}{2}(\sin 5t - \sin t)$

$$\therefore L(\sin 2t \cos 3t) = \frac{1}{2}L(\sin 5t - \sin t) = \frac{1}{2}[L(\sin 5t) - L(\sin t)]$$

$$= \frac{1}{2}[\frac{5}{s^2+5^2} - \frac{1}{s^2+1}] = \frac{2(s^2-5)}{(s^2+25)(s^2+1)}$$

(ii) Since $\sin 6t = 3\sin 2t - 4\sin^3 2t$

$$\implies \sin^3 2t = \frac{1}{4}[3\sin 2t - \sin 6t]$$

Now taking laplace transform both sides we have

$$L\sin^3 2t = \frac{1}{4}L[3\sin 2t - \sin 6t] = \frac{1}{4}[3L(\sin 2t) - L(\sin 6t)]$$

$$\therefore L\sin^3 2t = \frac{1}{4}[\frac{6}{s^2+2^2} - \frac{6}{s^2+6^2}] = \frac{48}{(s^2+4)(s^2+36)}$$

(iii) Taking laplace transform of the given function we have

$$L[7e^{2t} + 5\cos t + 7t^3 + 2] = 7L(e^{2t}) + 5L(\cos t) + 7L(t^3) + L(2)$$

$$= 7\frac{1}{s-2} + 5\frac{s}{s^2+1} + 7\frac{3!}{s^4} + 2\frac{1}{s} = \frac{7}{s-2} + \frac{5s}{s^2+1} + \frac{42}{s^4} + \frac{2}{s}$$

(iv) Since $(\sqrt{t} + \frac{1}{\sqrt{t}})^3 = t^{\frac{3}{2}} + t^{-\frac{3}{2}} + 3t^{\frac{1}{2}} + 3t^{-\frac{1}{2}}$

$$\therefore L(\sqrt{t}+\frac{1}{\sqrt{t}})^3 = L[t^{\frac{3}{2}}+t^{-\frac{3}{2}}+3t^{\frac{1}{2}}+3t^{-\frac{1}{2}}] = L(t^{\frac{3}{2}})+L(t^{-\frac{3}{2}})+3L(t^{\frac{1}{2}})+3L(t^{-\frac{1}{2}})$$

$$\implies L(\sqrt{t} + \frac{1}{\sqrt{t}})^3 = \frac{\Gamma\frac{5}{2}}{s^{\frac{5}{2}}} + \frac{\Gamma\frac{-1}{2}}{s^{-\frac{1}{2}}} + 3\frac{\Gamma\frac{3}{2}}{s^{\frac{3}{2}}} + 3\frac{\Gamma\frac{1}{2}}{s^{\frac{1}{2}}}$$

$$\implies L(\sqrt{t} + \frac{1}{\sqrt{t}})^3 = \sqrt{\pi}[\frac{3}{4s^{\frac{5}{2}}} - 2\sqrt{s} + \frac{3}{2s^{\frac{3}{2}}} + \frac{3}{s^{\frac{1}{2}}}]$$

[since $\Gamma(\frac{-1}{2}) = -2\sqrt{\pi}$ and $\Gamma\frac{1}{2} = \sqrt{\pi}$]

(v) Since $L[t^{-\frac{1}{2}}] = \frac{\Gamma\frac{1}{2}}{\sqrt{s}} = \frac{\sqrt{\pi}}{\sqrt{s}}$ $\quad [\because \Gamma\frac{1}{2} = \sqrt{\pi}]$

$$\therefore L[e^t t^{-\frac{1}{2}}] = \frac{\sqrt{\pi}}{\sqrt{(p-1)}} \qquad \text{[By using first shifting property]}$$

(vi) Since laplace transform of a function $f(t)$ is given by

$$L[f(t)] = \int_0^\infty e^{-st}f(t)dt$$

$$\implies L[f(t)] = \int_0^\pi e^{-st}\cos t dt + \int_\pi^\infty e^{-st}0.dt$$

$$\implies L[f(t)] = [\frac{e^{-st}}{s^2+1}(-s\cos t + \sin t)]_0^\pi = [\frac{e^{-s\pi}}{s^2+1}s - \frac{1}{s^2+1}(-s)]$$

$$\implies L[f(t)] = \frac{s(1+e^{-s\pi})}{s^2+1}$$

(vii) Since laplace transform of a function $f(t)$ is given by

$$L[f(t)] = \int_0^\infty e^{-st} f(t)dt$$

$$\Longrightarrow L[f(t)] = \int_0^1 e^{-st}dt + \int_1^2 e^{-st}.tdt + \int_2^\infty e^{-st}.t^2dt$$

$$\Longrightarrow L[f(t)] = (\tfrac{e^{-st}}{-s})_0^1 + (t.\tfrac{e^{-st}}{-s} - \tfrac{e^{-st}}{s^2})_1^2 + (t.\tfrac{e^{-st}}{-s})_2^\infty - \int_2^\infty 2t\tfrac{e^{-st}}{-s}dt$$

$$\Longrightarrow L[f(t)] = (\tfrac{1-e^{-s}}{s}) + (\tfrac{-2}{s}e^{-2s} - \tfrac{e^{-2s}}{s^2}) + (\tfrac{e^{-s}}{-s} - \tfrac{e^{-s}}{s^2}) + \tfrac{4}{s}e^{-2s} - \tfrac{2}{s}\int_2^\infty te^{-st}dt$$

$$\Longrightarrow L[f(t)] = \tfrac{1}{s} + \tfrac{2}{s}e^{-2s} + \tfrac{e^{-s}}{s^2} - \tfrac{e^{-2s}}{s^2} + \tfrac{2}{s}[(t\tfrac{e^{-st}}{-s})_2^\infty - \int_2^\infty \tfrac{e^{-st}}{-s}dt]$$

$$\Longrightarrow L[f(t)] = \tfrac{1}{s} + \tfrac{2}{s}e^{-2s} + \tfrac{e^{-s}}{s^2} + \tfrac{3e^{-2s}}{s^2} + \tfrac{2}{s^3}e^{-2s}$$

(viii) The laplace transform of the given funtion is

$$L[f(t)] = e^{-s\frac{\pi}{3}}L(\sin t) \qquad \text{[by second shifting property]}$$

$$L[f(t)] = e^{-s\frac{\pi}{3}}.\tfrac{1}{s^2+1}$$

Example 2 If $L(\cos^2 t) = \frac{s^2+2}{s(s^2+4)}$ then find $L(\cos^2 at)$.
Sol. Since we have $L(\cos^2 t) = \frac{s^2+2}{s(s^2+4)}$
Now by change of scale property we have

$$L(\cos^2 at) = \tfrac{1}{a}.\tfrac{(\frac{s}{a})^2+2}{\frac{s}{a}[(\frac{s}{a})^2+4]} = \tfrac{s^2+2a^2}{s(s^2+4a^2)}$$

Example 3 Find the laplace transform of $\sin\sqrt{t}$; hence find $L(\frac{\cos\sqrt{t}}{2\sqrt{t}})$.
Sol. Since by sine series expansion we have

$$\sin\sqrt{t} = \sqrt{t} - \tfrac{(\sqrt{t})^3}{3!} + \tfrac{(\sqrt{t})^5}{5!} - ....$$

$$\Longrightarrow = t^{\frac{1}{2}} - \tfrac{t^{\frac{3}{2}}}{3!} + \tfrac{t^{\frac{5}{2}}}{5!} - ....$$

$$\therefore L(\sin\sqrt{t}) = L(t^{\frac{1}{2}}) - L(\tfrac{t^{\frac{3}{2}}}{3!}) + L(\tfrac{t^{\frac{5}{2}}}{5!}) - ....$$

$$= \frac{\Gamma\frac{3}{2}}{s^{\frac{3}{2}}} - \frac{\Gamma\frac{5}{2}}{3!s^{\frac{5}{2}}} + \frac{\Gamma\frac{7}{2}}{5!s^{\frac{7}{2}}} - ....$$

$$= \tfrac{\sqrt{\pi}}{2s^{\frac{3}{2}}}[1 - (\tfrac{1}{2^2s}) + \tfrac{1}{2!}(\tfrac{1}{2^2s})^2 - ......]$$

$$\Longrightarrow L(\sin\sqrt{t}) = \frac{\sqrt{\pi}}{2s^{\frac{3}{2}}}e^{-\frac{1}{4s}}$$

Now

$$L[\tfrac{d}{dt}(\sin\sqrt{t})] = sL(\sin\sqrt{t}) - 0 \qquad \text{[by derivative property]}$$

$$L(\tfrac{\cos\sqrt{t}}{2\sqrt{t}}) = \frac{\sqrt{\pi}}{2s^{\frac{1}{2}}}e^{-\frac{1}{4s}}$$

Example 4 Obtain the laplace transform of $t^2e^t\sin 4t$.
Sol. Since $L(\sin 4t) = \frac{4}{s^2+16}$

$$L(e^t\sin 4t) = \frac{4}{(s-1)^2+16}$$

$$\text{and } L(te^t\sin 4t) = -\tfrac{d}{ds}[\tfrac{4}{(s-1)^2+16}] = -\tfrac{d}{ds}[\tfrac{4}{s^2-2s+17}] = \tfrac{4(2s-2)}{(s^2-2s+17)^2}$$

$$\Longrightarrow L(t^2e^t\sin 4t) = -\tfrac{d}{ds}[\tfrac{4(2s-2)}{(s^2-2s+17)^2}] = -4\tfrac{(s^2-2s+17)2-2(2s-2)^2}{(s^2-2s+17)^3}$$

$$\Longrightarrow L(t^2e^t\sin 4t) = 8\tfrac{(3s^2-6s-13)}{(s^2-2s+17)^3}$$

Example 5 Find laplace transform of $\int_0^t \frac{\sin at}{t}dt$.
Sol. Since $L(\sin at) = \frac{a}{s^2+a^2}$
So by division property we have

$$L(\tfrac{\sin at}{t}) = \int_s^\infty \tfrac{a}{s^2+a^2}ds = [\tan^{-1}\tfrac{s}{a}]_s^\infty = \tfrac{\pi}{2} - \tan^{-1}\tfrac{s}{a} = \cot^{-1}\tfrac{s}{a}$$

Thus by laplace transform of integral property we have

$$\int_0^t \tfrac{\sin at}{t}dt = \tfrac{1}{s}\cot^{-1}\tfrac{s}{a}.$$

Example 6 Find laplace transform of $\frac{\cos at-\cos bt}{t}$.
Sol. Since $L(\cos at - \cos bt) = L(\cos at) - L(\cos bt) = \frac{s}{s^2+a^2} - \frac{s}{s^2+b^2}$. Thus

$$L(\tfrac{\cos at-\cos bt}{t}) = \int_s^\infty[\tfrac{s}{s^2+a^2} - \tfrac{s}{s^2+b^2}]ds$$

$$\Longrightarrow L(\tfrac{\cos at-\cos bt}{t}) = [\tfrac{1}{2}\log(s^2+a^2) - \tfrac{1}{2}\log(s^2+b^2)]_s^\infty$$

$$\Longrightarrow L(\tfrac{\cos at-\cos bt}{t}) = [\tfrac{1}{2}\log(s^2+a^2) - \tfrac{1}{2}\log(s^2+b^2)]_s^\infty$$

$$\Longrightarrow L(\tfrac{\cos at-\cos bt}{t}) = \tfrac{1}{2}[\log\tfrac{s^2+a^2}{s^2+b^2}]_s^\infty = \tfrac{1}{2}[\log\tfrac{1+\frac{a^2}{s^2}}{1+\frac{b^2}{s^2}}]_s^\infty$$

$$\Longrightarrow L\left(\frac{\cos at-\cos bt}{t}\right)=\frac{1}{2}\log 1-\frac{1}{2}\log\frac{1+\frac{a^2}{s^2}}{1+\frac{b^2}{s^2}}$$

$$\Longrightarrow L\left(\frac{\cos at-\cos bt}{t}\right)=-\frac{1}{2}\log\frac{s^2+a^2}{s^2+b^2}=\frac{1}{2}\log\frac{s^2+b^2}{s^2+a^2}\qquad[\therefore \log 1=0]$$

Example 7 Find laplace transform of $\frac{1-\cos t}{t^2}$.
Sol. Since $L(1-\cos t)=L(1)-L(\cos t)=\frac{1}{s}-\frac{s}{s^2+1}$. So

$$L\left(\frac{1-\cos t}{t}\right)=\int_s^\infty\left[\frac{1}{s}-\frac{s}{s^2+1}\right]ds=\left[\log s-\frac{1}{2}\log(s^2+1)\right]_s^\infty$$

$$L\left(\frac{1-\cos t}{t}\right)=\frac{1}{2}[\log s^2-\log(s^2+1)]_s^\infty=\frac{1}{2}\left[\log\frac{s^2}{s^2+1}\right]_s^\infty$$

$$L\left(\frac{1-\cos t}{t}\right)=\frac{1}{2}\left[\log\frac{1}{1+\frac{1}{s^2}}\right]_s^\infty=-\frac{1}{2}\log\frac{s^2}{s^2+1}$$

Again

$$L\left(\frac{1-\cos t}{t^2}\right)=-\frac{1}{2}\int_s^\infty\log\frac{s^2}{s^2+1}ds=-\frac{1}{2}\int_s^\infty\left(\log\frac{s^2}{s^2+1}.1\right)ds$$

Integrating by parts, we have

$$L\left(\frac{1-\cos t}{t^2}\right)=-\frac{1}{2}\left[\log\frac{s^2}{s^2+1}.s-\int\frac{s^2+1}{s^2}.\frac{(s^2+1).2s-s^2.2s}{(s^2+1)^2}.sds\right]_s^\infty$$

$$L\left(\frac{1-\cos t}{t^2}\right)=-\frac{1}{2}\left[s\log\frac{s^2}{s^2+1}-2\tan^{-1}s\right]_s^\infty$$

$$L\left(\frac{1-\cos t}{t^2}\right)=-\frac{1}{2}\left[-\pi-s\log\frac{s^2}{s^2+1}+2\tan^{-1}s\right]$$

$$L\left(\frac{1-\cos t}{t^2}\right)=\frac{\pi}{2}+\frac{s}{2}\log\frac{s^2}{s^2+1}-\tan^{-1}s=\cot^{-1}s+\frac{s}{2}\log\frac{s^2}{s^2+1}.$$

Example 8 Express thc following function in terms of unit step function:

$$f(t)=\begin{cases}t-1, & 1<t<2\\ 3-t & 2<t<3\end{cases}$$

and find its laplace transform.
Sol. The given function can be rewritten as

$$f(t)=(t-1)[u(t-1)-u(t-2)]+(3-t)[u(t-2)-u(t-3)]$$

$$=(t-1)u(t-1)-(t-1)u(t-2)+(3-t)u(t-2)+(t-3)u(t-3)$$

$$= (t-1)u(t-1) - 2(t-2)u(t-2) + (t-3)u(t-3)$$

$$= e^{-s}L(t) - 2e^{-2s}L(t) - e^{-3s}L(t) \qquad \text{[by second shifting property]}$$

$$L[f(t)] = \frac{e^{-s}}{s^2} - 2\frac{e^{-2s}}{s^2} + \frac{e^{-3s}}{s^2}.$$

Example 9 A function $f(t)$ obeys the equation $f(t) + 2\int_0^t f(t)dt = \cosh 2t$. Find the laplace transform of the function $f(t)$.
Sol. Since the given equation be the

$$f(t) + 2\int_0^t f(t)dt = \cosh 2t$$

Taking laplace transform of above equation we have

$$L[f(t)] + 2L[\int_0^t f(t)dt] = L[\cosh 2t]$$

By using property of laplace transform of Integral, we have

$$F(s) + 2\frac{1}{s}F(s) = \frac{s}{s^2-4}$$

where $F(s)$ is laplace transform of $f(t)$.

$$F(s)[1 + \frac{2}{s}] = \frac{s}{s^2-4} \qquad \Longrightarrow F(s)[\frac{s+2}{s}] = \frac{s}{s^2-4}$$

$$\Longrightarrow F(s) = \frac{s^2}{(s^2-4)(s+2)}$$

Example 10 Find the laplace transform of the periodic function:

$$f(t) = \begin{cases} t, & 0 < t < \pi \\ \pi - t & \pi < t < 2\pi \end{cases}$$

Sol. The given function is periodic with period $2\pi = T$
So laplace transform of periodic function is given by

$$L[f(t)] = \frac{\int_0^T e^{-st} f(t)dt}{1-e^{-sT}} = \frac{1}{1-e^{-2\pi s}}[\int_0^\pi e^{-st}tdt + \int_\pi^{2\pi} e^{-st}(\pi - t)dt]$$

$$= \frac{1}{1-e^{-2\pi s}}[(\frac{te^{-st}}{-s} - \frac{e^{-st}}{(-s)^2})_0^\pi + (\frac{(\pi-t)e^{-st}}{-s} - (-1)\frac{e^{-st}}{(-s)^2})_\pi^{2\pi}]$$

$$= \frac{1}{1-e^{-2\pi s}}[-\frac{\pi e^{-\pi s}}{s} - \frac{e^{-\pi s}}{s^2} + \frac{1}{s^2} + \pi\frac{e^{-2\pi s}}{s} + \frac{e^{-2\pi s}}{s^2} - 0 - \frac{e^{-\pi s}}{s^2}]$$

$$= \frac{1}{1-e^{-2\pi s}}[\frac{\pi}{s}(e^{-2\pi s} - e^{-\pi s}) + \frac{1}{s^2}(1 + e^{-2\pi s} - 2e^{-\pi s})]$$

$$L[f(t)] = \frac{-\pi s e^{-\pi s} + 1 - e^{-\pi s}}{s^2(1+e^{-\pi s})}$$

Example 11 Find the laplace transform of the periodic function:

$$f(t) = \begin{cases} \sin at, & 0 < t < \pi/a \\ 0 & \pi/a < t < 2\pi/a \end{cases}$$

Sol. The given function is periodic with period $2\pi/a = T$
So laplace transform of periodic function is given by

$$L[f(t)] = \frac{\int_0^T e^{-st} f(t)dt}{1-e^{-sT}} = \frac{1}{1-e^{-2\pi s/a}}[\int_0^{\pi/a} e^{-st} \sin at dt + \int_{\pi/a}^{2\pi/a} e^{-st}.0dt]$$

$$L[f(t)] = \frac{1}{1-e^{-2\pi s/a}}[\frac{e^{-st}(-s\sin at - a\cos at)}{s^2+a^2}]_0^{\pi/a}$$

$$[\text{since} \int e^{at} \sin bt dt = \frac{e^{at}(a\sin bt - b\cos bt)}{a^2+b^2}]$$

$$L[f(t)] = \frac{1}{1-e^{-2\pi s/a}}[\frac{ae^{-\pi s/a}+a}{s^2+a^2}] = \frac{a(1+e^{-\pi s/a})}{(s^2+a^2)(1-e^{-\pi s/a})(1+e^{-\pi s/a})}$$

$$\implies L[f(t)] = \frac{a}{(s^2+a^2)(1-e^{-\pi s/a})}$$

Example 12 Find the laplace transform of the periodic function:

$$f(t) = \begin{cases} t, & 0 < t < a \\ 2a - t & a < t < 2a \end{cases}$$

Sol. The given function is periodic with period $2a = T$
So laplace transform of periodic function is given by

$$L[f(t)] = \frac{\int_0^T e^{-st} f(t)dt}{1-e^{-sT}} = \frac{1}{1-e^{-2as}}[\int_0^a e^{-st} t dt + \int_a^{2a} e^{-st}(2a - t)dt]$$

$$= \frac{1}{1-e^{-2as}}[(\frac{te^{-st}}{-s} - \frac{e^{-st}}{(-s)^2})_0^a + (\frac{(2a-t)e^{-st}}{-s} - (-1)\frac{e^{-st}}{(-s)^2})_a^{2a}]$$

$$= \frac{1}{1-e^{-2as}}[-\frac{ae^{-as}}{s} - \frac{e^{-as}}{s^2} + \frac{1}{s^2} + a\frac{e^{-as}}{s} + \frac{e^{-2as}}{s^2} - \frac{e^{-as}}{s^2}]$$

$$= \frac{1}{1-e^{-2as}}[\frac{1}{s^2}(1 + e^{-2as} - 2e^{-as})]$$

$$= \frac{1}{s^2}\frac{(1-e^{-as})^2}{(1+e^{-as})(1-e^{-as})} = \frac{1}{s^2}[\frac{1-e^{-as}}{1+e^{-as}}] = \frac{1}{s^2}[\frac{e^{as/2}-e^{-as/2}}{e^{as/2}+e^{-as/2}}]$$

Thus we have $L[f(t)] = \frac{1}{s^2}\tanh\frac{as}{2}$.

1.5 Laplace Transform of special function

1. Lapalce transform of Unit Step Function or Heaviside's unit function

Since unit step function is given by

$$f(t) = \begin{cases} 0, & t < a \\ 1 & t \geq a \end{cases}$$

Taking laplace transform of above function

$$L[u(t-a)] = \int_0^\infty e^{-st} u(t-a) dt$$

$$= \int_0^a e^{-st}.0dt + \int_a^\infty e^{-st}.1dt$$

$$L[u(t-a)] = (\frac{e^{-st}}{-s})_a^\infty = \frac{e^{-as}}{s}$$

2. Laplace transform of exponential integral function $\int_t^\infty \frac{e^{-x}}{x} dx$

Let $f(t) = \int_t^\infty \frac{e^{-x}}{x} dx$
$\implies f'(t) = -\frac{e^{-t}}{t} \implies tf'(t) = -e^{-t}$
Here $-ve$ sign appears due to lower limit.

Taking laplace transform of $tf'(t)$, we have

$$L[tf'(t)] = L[-e^{-t}] = -L[e^{-t}]$$

$$\implies -\frac{d}{ds}[sF(s) - f(0)] = -\frac{1}{s+1}$$

$$\frac{d}{ds}[sF(s)] = \frac{1}{s+1} \qquad [\because f(0) = \text{constant}, \quad \therefore \frac{d}{ds} f(0) = 0 \ ].$$

Integrating both sides we get

$$sF(s) = \log(s+1) + c \tag{1.5}$$

taking limit $s \to 0$ both side of the above equation we have

$$\lim_{s \to 0} sF(s) = \lim_{s \to 0} [\log(s+1) + c] = 0 + c = c \tag{1.6}$$

Again using limit $t \to \infty$ in the equation $f(t) = \int_t^\infty \frac{e^{-x}}{x} dx$ we have

$$\lim_{t\to\infty} f(t) = \lim_{t\to\infty} \int_t^\infty \frac{e^{-x}}{x} dx = 0 \qquad (1.7)$$

Now using final value theorem $\lim_{s\to 0} sF(s) = \lim_{t\to\infty} f(t)$ between equation (1.6) and (1.7), we have $c = 0$. Now using this value of c in equation (1.5), we have

$$sF(s) = \log(s+1) \implies F(s) = \frac{\log(s+1)}{s}$$

Thus we have

$$L[\int_t^\infty \frac{e^{-x}}{x} dx] = \frac{\log(s+1)}{s}.$$

3. Laplace transform of error function

Since the error function is given by

$$erf\ \sqrt{t} = \frac{2}{\sqrt{\pi}} \int_0^{\sqrt{t}} e^{-x^2} dx \qquad (1.8)$$

Now taking laplace transform of above equation we have

$$L[erf\ \sqrt{t}] = L[\tfrac{2}{\sqrt{\pi}} \int_0^{\sqrt{t}} e^{-x^2} dx]$$

$$\implies = \tfrac{2}{\sqrt{\pi}} L[\int_0^{\sqrt{t}} (1 - x^2 + \tfrac{x^4}{2!} - \tfrac{x^6}{3!} + ...) dx]$$

$$\implies = \tfrac{2}{\sqrt{\pi}} L[(x - \tfrac{x^3}{3} + \tfrac{x^5}{10} - \tfrac{x^7}{42} + ...)_0^{\sqrt{t}}]$$

$$\implies = \tfrac{2}{\sqrt{\pi}} L[(t^{1/2} - \tfrac{t^{3/2}}{3} + \tfrac{t^{5/2}}{10} - \tfrac{t^{7/2}}{42} + ...)]$$

$$\implies = \tfrac{2}{\sqrt{\pi}} [\tfrac{\Gamma 3/2}{s^{3/2}} - \tfrac{\Gamma 5/2}{3s^{5/2}} + \tfrac{\Gamma 7/2}{10s^{7/2}} - \tfrac{\Gamma 9/2}{42s^{9/2}} + ...]$$

$$\implies = \tfrac{1}{s^{3/2}} - \tfrac{1}{2}\tfrac{1}{s^{5/2}} + \tfrac{1}{2}\tfrac{3}{4}\tfrac{1}{s^{7/2}} - \tfrac{1}{2}\tfrac{3}{4}\tfrac{5}{6}\tfrac{1}{s^{9/2}} + ...$$

$$\implies = \tfrac{1}{s^{3/2}}[1 - \tfrac{1}{2}\tfrac{1}{s} + \tfrac{1}{2}\tfrac{3}{4}\tfrac{1}{s^2} - \tfrac{1}{2}\tfrac{3}{4}\tfrac{5}{6}\tfrac{1}{s^3} + ...]$$

$$\implies = \tfrac{1}{s^{3/2}}[1 - \tfrac{1}{2}\tfrac{1}{s} + \tfrac{(-1/2)(-3/2)}{2!}\tfrac{1}{s^2} - \tfrac{(-1/2)(-3/2)(-5/2)}{2!}\tfrac{1}{s^3} + ...]$$

$$\Longrightarrow = \frac{1}{s^{3/2}}[1+\frac{1}{s}]^{-1/2} = \frac{1}{s^{3/2}}[\frac{s}{s+1}]^{-1/2} = \frac{1}{s\sqrt{(s+1)}}$$

Thus

$$L[erf\ \sqrt{t}] = \frac{1}{s\sqrt{(s+1)}}$$

4. Laplace transform of Complementary error function

Since the complementary error function given by

$$erf_c\ \sqrt{t} = 1 - erf\ \sqrt{t}$$

Taking laplace transform of above equation, we have

$$L[erf_c\ \sqrt{t}] = L[1 - erf\ \sqrt{t}] = L[1] - L[erf\ \sqrt{t}]$$

$$= \frac{1}{s} - \frac{1}{s\sqrt{(s+1)}} = \frac{\sqrt{(s+1)}-1}{s\sqrt{(s+1)}} = \frac{(\sqrt{(s+1)}-1)(\sqrt{(s+1)}+1)}{s\sqrt{(s+1)}(\sqrt{(s+1)}+1)}$$

$$L[erf_c\ \sqrt{t}] = \frac{1}{\sqrt{(s+1)}(\sqrt{(s+1)}+1)}$$

5. Laplace transform of Dirac's delta function or unit impulse function

Consider a function $\delta_\epsilon(t)$ given by

$$\delta_\epsilon(t) = \begin{cases} 0, & if \quad t < 0 \\ 1/\epsilon, & if \quad 0 < t < \epsilon \\ 0, & if \quad t > \epsilon \end{cases} \tag{1.9}$$

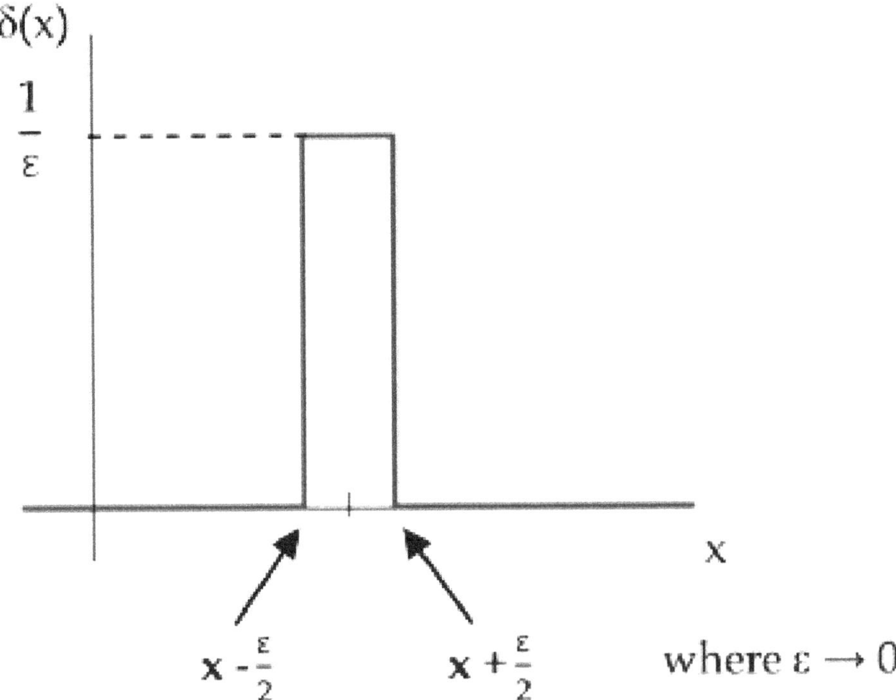

Fig 3: Dirac's delta function

The Dirac's delta function is denoted by $\delta(t)$ and defined as

$$\delta(t) = \lim_{\epsilon \to 0} \delta_\epsilon(t) \tag{1.10}$$

Taking laplace transform of equation (1.10) we have

$$L[\delta(t)] = \lim_{\epsilon \to 0} L[\delta_\epsilon(t)]$$

Using equation (1.9) in above equation we have

$$L[\delta(t)] = \lim_{\epsilon \to 0}[\int_0^\epsilon e^{-st}\tfrac{1}{\epsilon}dt + \int_\epsilon^\infty e^{-st}.0dt]$$

$$\implies \quad L[\delta(t)] = \lim_{\epsilon \to 0}[\tfrac{1}{\epsilon}[-\tfrac{e^{-st}}{s}]_0^\epsilon] = \lim_{\epsilon \to 0}[\tfrac{1-e^{-s\epsilon}}{s\epsilon}]$$

$$\implies \quad L[\delta(t)] = \tfrac{1}{s}\lim_{\epsilon \to 0}\tfrac{se^{-s\epsilon}}{1} \qquad \text{[By L Hopital's rule]}$$

$$\Longrightarrow \qquad L[\delta(t)] = \tfrac{1}{s}.s = 1. \qquad\qquad [\text{since } \lim_{\epsilon\to 0} e^{-s\epsilon} = 1]$$

Thus laplace transform of dirac delta function is given by

$$L[\delta(t)] = 1.$$

6. Laplace transform of Bessel function

The Bessel function of order n is denoted by $J_n(t)$ and defined as

$$J_n(t) = \sum_{r=0}^{\infty} \frac{(-1)^r}{r!\Gamma(n+r+1)} (\frac{t}{2})^{n+2r} \qquad (1.11)$$

Now put $n = 0$ in above equation we have

$$J_0(t) = \sum_{r=0}^{\infty} \tfrac{(-1)^r}{r!\Gamma(r+1)} (\tfrac{t}{2})^{2r}$$

$$\Longrightarrow = 1 - \tfrac{t^2}{2^2} + \tfrac{t^4}{2^2.4^2} - \tfrac{t^6}{2^2.4^2 6^2} + ...$$

Taking laplace transform of above equation we have

$$L[J_0(t)] = \tfrac{1}{s} - \tfrac{1}{2^2} \tfrac{2!}{s^3} + \tfrac{1}{2^2 4^2} \tfrac{4!}{s^5} - frac1 2^2 4^2 6^2 \tfrac{6!}{s^7} + ...$$

$$\Longrightarrow = \tfrac{1}{s}[1 - \tfrac{1}{2}\tfrac{1}{s^2} + \tfrac{1}{2}\tfrac{3}{4}(\tfrac{1}{s^2})^2 - \tfrac{1}{2}\tfrac{3}{4}\tfrac{5}{6}(\tfrac{1}{s^2})^3 + ...]$$

$$\Longrightarrow = \tfrac{1}{s}(1 + \tfrac{1}{s^2})^{-1/2} = \tfrac{1}{\sqrt{(1+s^2)}}$$

Thus

$$L[J_0(t)] = \tfrac{1}{\sqrt{(1+s^2)}}$$

Similarilay we have

$$L[J_1(t)] = 1 - \tfrac{s}{\sqrt{(1+s^2)}}$$

and so on.

Example 13 If $L[erf\ \sqrt{t}] = \frac{1}{s\sqrt{(s+1)}}$ then find $L[erf\ 2\sqrt{t}]$ and $L[t.erf\ 2\sqrt{t}]$.

Sol. Since $L[erf\ \sqrt{t}] = \frac{1}{s\sqrt{(s+1)}}$ then

$$L[erf\ 2\sqrt{t}] = L[erf\ \sqrt{4t}] = \tfrac{1}{4}.\tfrac{1}{s/4\sqrt{(\frac{s}{4}+1)}} \qquad [\text{By change of scale property}]$$

$$\implies L[erf\ 2\sqrt{t}] = \frac{2}{s\sqrt{(s+4)}}$$

Again

$$L[t.erf\ 2\sqrt{t}] = -\frac{d}{ds}(\frac{2}{s\sqrt{(s+4)}}) \quad \text{[By Multiplication by t property]}$$

$$\implies L[t.erf\ 2\sqrt{t}] = \frac{3s+8}{s^2(s+4)^{3/2}}.$$

Example 14 If $L[J_1(t)] = 1 - \frac{s}{\sqrt{(1+s^2)}}$ then find $L[t.J_1(t)]$.

Sol. Since $L[J_1(t)] = 1 - \frac{s}{\sqrt{(1+s^2)}}$ then

$$L[t.J_1(t)] = -\frac{d}{ds}(1 - \frac{s}{\sqrt{(1+s^2)}}) \quad \text{[By Multiplication by t property]}$$

$$\implies L[t.J_1(t)] = \frac{1}{(s^2+1)^{3/2}}$$

1.6 Evaluation of Integrals by using Laplace transforms

Example 15 Evaluate $\int_0^\infty te^{-2t}\cos t dt$.

Sol. Since $L[\cos t] = \frac{s}{s^2+1}$ then

$$L(t.\cos t) = -\frac{d}{ds}\frac{s}{s^2+1} = \frac{s^2-1}{(s^2+1)^2} \quad \text{[By multiplication with t property]}$$

$$\implies \int_0^\infty e^{-st}t.\cos t dt = \frac{s^2-1}{(s^2+1)^2} \quad \text{[By definition of laplace transform]}$$

Taking limit as $s \to 2$, in above equation we have

$$\implies \int_0^\infty e^{-2t}t.\cos t dt = \frac{2^2-1}{(2^2+1)^2} = \frac{4-1}{(4+1)^2} = \frac{3}{25}$$

Example 16 Show that $\int_0^\infty \frac{\sin t}{t} dt = \frac{\pi}{2}$.

Sol. Since $L(\sin t) = \frac{1}{s^2+1}$, then

$$L(\sin t/t) = \int_s^\infty \frac{1}{s^2+1} ds \quad \text{[By division property]}$$

$$\implies L(\sin t/t) = [\tan^{-1} s]_s^\infty = \tan^{-1}\infty - \tan^{-1} s$$

$$\implies L(\sin t/t) = \frac{\pi}{2} - \tan^{-1} s$$

$$\implies \int_0^\infty e^{-st}(\sin t/t) = \frac{\pi}{2} - \tan^{-1} s \quad \text{[By definition of lapalce transform]}$$

Taking limit as $s \to 0$, in above equation we have

$$\int_0^\infty e^0(\sin t/t) = \frac{\pi}{2} - \tan^{-1} 0$$

$$\implies \int_0^\infty (\sin t/t) = \frac{\pi}{2} \quad \text{[since } e^0 = 1 \text{ and } \tan^{-1} 0 = 0\text{]}.$$

1.7 Miscellaneous Exercise

1. Find laplace transform of following functions:
$i.\ (t^2+1)^2$ $ii.\ \sin^2 at$ $iii.\ \sin\sqrt{t}$ $iv.\ 1/\sqrt{\pi t}$ $v.\ (\sin t-\cos t)^2$
Ans. $i.\ \frac{24+4s^2+s^4}{s^5}$ $ii.\ \dfrac{2a^2}{s(s^2+4a^2)}$ $iii.\ \frac{\sqrt{\pi}}{2s^{3/2}}e^{-1/4s}$ $iv.\ 1/\sqrt{s}$ $v.\ \frac{s^2-2s+4}{s(s^2+4)}$
2. Find laplace transform of following functions:
$i.\ e^{-3t}\sin 2t$ $ii.\ \sinh at\cos at$ $iii.\ e^{-t}\sin^2 t$ $iv.\ (e^{-at}t^{n-1})/(n-1)!$
Ans. $i.\ 2/[(s+3)^2+4]$ $ii\ \frac{a(s^2-2a^2)}{s^4+4a^4}$ $iii.\ 2/(s+1)(s^2+2s+5)$ $iv.\ 1/(s+a)^n$
3. Given that $L[2\sqrt{\frac{t}{\pi}}]=1/s^{3/2}$ then prove that $L[1/\sqrt{\pi t}]=1/s^{1/2}$.
4. Find the laplace transform of following functions:
$i.\ t^2\sin at$ $ii.\ t^ne^{at}$ $iii.\ t^3\cos t$ $iv.\ (t^2-3t+2)\sin at$
Ans. $i.\ \frac{2a(3s^2-a^2)}{(s^2+a^2)^3}$ $ii.\ \frac{n!}{(s-a)^{n+1}}$ $iii.\ (6s^4-36s^2+6)/(s^2+1)^4$ $iv.\ (6s^4-18s^3+126s^2-162s+432)/(s^2+9)^3$
5. Find the laplace transform of $\sin at/t$. Does the laplace transform of $\cos at/t$ exist.
Ans. $L(\sin at/t)=\cot^{-1}\frac{s}{a}$ $L(\cos at/t)=$Does not exist.
6. Prove that $L(\sin^2 t/t)=\frac{1}{4}\log\frac{s^2+4}{s^2}$.
7. Find $L[F(t)]$ if $F(t)$ is given by $F(t)=\int_0^\infty \cos tx^2dx$.
Ans. $\frac{\pi}{2\sqrt{2s}}$.
8. Let $f(t)$ be a periodic function with period 4, where

$$f(t)=\begin{cases}3t, & 0<t<2\\ 6, & 2<t<4\end{cases}$$

then prove that $L[f(t)]=\frac{3(1-e^{-2s}-2se^{-4s})}{s^2(1-e^{-4s})}$.
9. Let $f(t)$ be a periodic function with period 2π, where

$$f(t)=\begin{cases}\sin t, & 0<t<\pi\\ 0, & \pi<t<2\pi\end{cases}$$

then prove that $L[f(t)]=\frac{1}{(s^2+1)(1-e^{-s\pi})}$.
10. If $f(t)=t^2$, $0<t<2$ and $f(t+2)=f(t)$ then find $L[f(t)]$.
Ans. $[2-(4s^2+4s+2)]/s^3(1-e^{-2s})$.
11. Evaluate $L[\int_0^t\frac{\sin x}{x}dx]$.
Ans. $\frac{1}{s}\tan^{-1}\frac{1}{s}$.
12. Prove that $L[e^{3t}erf\ \sqrt{t}]=1/(s-3)\sqrt{(s-2)}$.

13. Show that $L[f(t)] = e^{-as/(s-1)}$ where $f(t)$ is given by $f(t) = \begin{cases} e^{t-a}, & t > a \\ 0, & t < 0 \end{cases}$.

14. Find laplace transform of following functions:

i. $f(t) = \begin{cases} \cos(t - 2\pi/3), & t > 2\pi/3 \\ 0, & t < 2\pi/3 \end{cases}$

ii. $f(t) = \begin{cases} \sin(t - 2\pi/3), & t > \pi/3 \\ 0, & t < \pi/3 \end{cases}$

iii. $f(t) = \begin{cases} \sin(t - 2\pi/3), & t > 2\pi/3 \\ 0, & t < 2\pi/3 \end{cases}$.

Ans. *i.* $e^{-2\pi s/3}\frac{s}{(s^2+1)}$ *ii.* $\frac{e^{-\pi s/3}}{(s^2+1)}$ *iii.* $\frac{e^{-2\pi s/3}}{(s^2+1)}$

15. Evaluate following integrals:

i. $\int_0^\infty \frac{e^{-t}-e^{-3t}}{t}dt$ *ii.* $\int_0^\infty \frac{e^{-at}-e^{-bt}}{t}dt$ *iii.* $\int_0^\infty te^{-3t}\sin t dt$ *iv.* $\int_0^\infty t^3 e^{-t}\sin t dt$

Ans. *i.* $\log 3$ *ii.* $\log\frac{b}{a}$ *iii.* $3/50$ *iv.* 0.

16. Prove that $\int_0^\infty \frac{\sin^2 t}{t^2}dt = \frac{\pi}{2}$.

17. Prove that $\int_0^t e^{-2t} t \sin^3 t dt = \frac{3(s+2)}{2s}\left[\frac{1}{[(s+2)^2+9]^2} - \frac{1}{[(s+2)^2+1]^2}\right]$.

18. Show that $L[\frac{1-\cos t}{t^2}] = \cot^{-1} s + \frac{s}{2}\log\frac{s^2}{s^2+1}$.

19. Express the following function

$$f(t) = \begin{cases} 0, & 0 < t < 1 \\ t - 1, & 1 < t < 2 \\ 1, & 2 < t \end{cases}$$

in terms of unit step function and find its laplace transform.

Ans. $L[f(t)] = \frac{e^{-s}}{s^2} - \frac{e^{-2s}}{s^2}$.

20. Show that $L[f(t)] = \frac{1}{s}\tanh\frac{as}{4}$ where $f(t)$ is a periodic function and given by

$$f(t) = \begin{cases} 1, & 0 \le t \le a/2 \\ -1, & a/2 \le t < a \end{cases}$$

21. Evaluate following functions:

i. $\int_0^\infty t^2 e^{3t}\sin^2 t dt$ *ii.* $\int_0^\infty \frac{e^{-2t}\sinh t \sin t}{t}dt$ *iii.* $\int_0^\infty te^{-4t}\sin t dt$

Ans. *i.* $-\frac{2440}{59319}$ *ii.* $\frac{1}{2}\tan^{-1}\frac{1}{2}$ *iii.* $\frac{8}{289}$.

22. Show that $L[f(t)] = \frac{2}{Ts^2}\tanh\frac{sT}{4} - \frac{1}{s(e^{sT/2}+1)}$ where $f(t)$ is a periodic function with period T and given by

$$f(t) = \begin{cases} 2t/T, & 0 \le t \le T/2 \\ \frac{2}{T}(T-t), & T/2 \le t < T \end{cases}$$

23. Find the laplace transform of following periodic function:

$$f(t) = \begin{cases} t, & 0 < t \le a \\ 2a - t, & a < t < 2a \end{cases}$$

Ans. $\frac{1}{s^2} \tanh \frac{as}{2}$
24. Show that $L[\frac{1}{t}e^{-t}\sin t] = \cot^{-1}(s+1)$.
25. Prove that $L[\frac{1}{t}\sinh t] = -\frac{1}{2}\log\frac{s-1}{s+1}$.
26. Show that $L[\frac{e^{at}-\cos bt}{t}] = \frac{1}{2}\log\frac{s^2+b^2}{(s-a)^2}$.
27. Find the laplace transform of $4\cosh 2t \sin 4t$.
Ans. $-i[\frac{4+8i}{s^2-(2+4i)^2} - \frac{4-8i}{s^2-(2-4i)^2}]$.
28. Show that $L[\frac{1}{2a^3}(\sin at - at\cos at)] = \frac{1}{(s^2+a^2)^2}$.
29. Show that $L[\frac{1}{2a}(\sin at + at\cos at)] = \frac{s^2}{(s^2+a^2)^2}$.

Chapter 2

Inverse Laplace Transform

2.1 Introduction

If $F(s)$ is the Laplace transform of a function $f(t)$, then $f(t)$ is referred to as the inverse Laplace transform.

In this case, if $L[f(t)] = F(s)$, then $L^{-1}[F(s)] = f(t)$, where L^{-1} denotes the inverse Laplace transform operator.

From an application perspective, the inverse Laplace transform is highly useful for solving ordinary linear differential equations with constant coefficients, simultaneous differential equations, and problems in electric circuits, all without the need to find the general solution or arbitrary constants.

To find the inverse Laplace transform of a given function, we attempt to recognize the function in a form similar to a standard expression whose inverse is a known standard function. Alternatively, we can decompose the given function of s into a series of simpler expressions (using partial fractions), which can then be compared to standard functions of s whose inverse Laplace transforms are known.

Let us begin by listing the inverse Laplace transforms of some standard elementary functions and related functions. The table provided will serve as a handy reference, particularly for solving differential equations using Laplace transforms.

Sr. No.	Laplace transform of [F(s)]	Inverse Laplace Transform f(t)
1.	1/s	1
2.	$\frac{1}{s-a}$	e^{at}
3.	$\frac{1}{s^n}$	$\frac{tn-1}{(n-1)!}$, for $n = 0, 1, 2, ...$
		otherwise $\frac{t^{n-1}}{\Gamma n}$
4.	$\frac{1}{s^2+a^2}$	$\frac{1}{a}\sin at$
5.	$\frac{s}{s^2+a^2}$	$\cos at$
6.	$\frac{1}{s^2-a^2}$	$\frac{1}{a}\sinh at$
7.	$\frac{s}{s^2-a^2}$	$\cosh at$
8.	$F(s-a)$	$e^{at}f(t)$
9.	$\frac{1}{(s-a)^2+b^2}$	$\frac{1}{b}e^{at}\sin bt$
10.	$\frac{s-a}{(s-a)^2+b^2}$	$e^{at}\cos at$
11.	$\frac{1}{(s-a)^2-b^2}$	$\frac{1}{b}e^{at}\sinh bt$
12.	$\frac{s-a}{(s-a)^2-b^2}$	$e^{at}\cosh bt$
13.	$\frac{1}{(s^2+a^2)^2}$	$\frac{1}{2a^3}(\sin at - at\cos at)$
14.	$\frac{s^2}{(s^2+a^2)^2}$	$\frac{1}{2a}(\sin at + at\cos at)$
15.	$\frac{s}{(s^2+a^2)^2}$	$\frac{1}{2a}t\sin at$
16.	$\frac{s^2-a^2}{(s^2+a^2)^2}$	$t\cos at$

2.2 Properties of Inverse laplace transform

Important properties of inverse laplace transform are given below:

Sr. No.	Name of property	Function F(s)=L[f(t)]	$L^{-1}F(s) = f(t)$
1.	Linear	$aF(s) + bG(s)$	$af(t) + bg(t)$
2.	First Shifting	$F(s + a)$	$e^{-at}f(t)$
3.	Second Shifting	$e^{-as}F(s)$	$f(t-a)u(t-a)$
4.	Derivative	$\frac{d}{ds}F(s)$	$-tf(t)$
5.	Multiplication by s	$sF(s)$	$\frac{d}{dt}f(t) + f(0)\delta(t)$
6.	Integral of a function	$\int_s^\infty F(s)ds$	$\frac{f(t)}{t}$
7.	Division by s	$\frac{F(s)}{s}$	$\int_0^t f(t)dt$
8.	Convolution theorem	$F(s).G(s)$	$f(t) * g(t) = \int_0^t f(x)g(t-x)dx$

Note: 1. When a fraction is in improper fraction then Inverse Laplace transform is not possible.

2. A fraction $[F(s) = \frac{G(s)}{H(s)}]$ is said to be improper fraction if degree of $G(s)$ is greater or equal to the degree of $H(s)$.

2.3 Solved Problems

Example 1 Show that $\frac{1}{s^{1/2}} = L[\frac{1}{\sqrt{\pi t}}]$.

Sol. Since we known that $L^{-1}[\frac{1}{s^n}] = \frac{t^{n-1}}{(n-1)!} = \frac{t^{n-1}}{\Gamma n}$

So we have

$$L^{-1}[\frac{1}{s^{1/2}}] = \frac{t^{(1/2)-1}}{\Gamma 1/2} = \frac{t^{-1/2}}{\sqrt{\pi}} = \frac{1}{\sqrt{\pi t}} \qquad [\text{since } \Gamma 1/2 = \sqrt{\pi}]$$

$$\implies \frac{1}{s^{1/2}} = L[\frac{1}{\sqrt{\pi t}}].$$

Example 2 Find the inverse laplace transform of following functions:

$i.\ \frac{s}{s^2-16}$ $\quad ii.\ \frac{s-1}{(s-1)^2+4}$ $\quad iii.\ \frac{1}{s^2-3s+3}$ $\quad iv.\ \frac{s^2+2s+6}{s^3}$ $\quad v.\ \frac{s-2}{6s^2+20}$.

Sol. i. $L^{-1}\frac{s}{s^2-16} = L^{-1}\frac{s}{s^2-4^2} = \cosh 4t$

ii. $L^{-1}\frac{s-1}{(s-1)^2+4} = e^t L^{-1}\frac{s}{s^2+4}$ [by first shifting property of inverse laplace transform]

$$\implies \quad L^{-1}\frac{s-1}{(s-1)^2+4} = e^t \cos 2t$$

iii. The given function can be written as

$$L^{-1}\frac{1}{s^2-3s+3} = L^{-1}[\frac{1}{(s-3/2)^2+3/4}] = \frac{2}{\sqrt{3}}e^{3t/2}\sin\frac{\sqrt{3}}{2}t$$

iv. Here we have

$$L^{-1}\frac{s^2+2s+6}{s^3} = L^{-1}[\frac{1}{s}+\frac{2}{s^2}+\frac{6}{s^3}] = 1+\frac{2t}{1!}+\frac{6t^2}{2!} = 1+2t+3t^2.$$

v. Here we have

$$L^{-1}\frac{s-2}{6s^2+20} = L^{-1}\frac{s}{6s^2+20} - L^{-1}\frac{2}{6s^2+20} = \frac{1}{6}L^{-1}\frac{s}{s^2+10/3} - \frac{1}{3}L^{-1}\frac{1}{s^2+10/3}$$

$$\implies \quad L^{-1}\frac{s-2}{6s^2+20} = \frac{1}{6}\cos\sqrt{\frac{10}{3}}t - \frac{1}{3}\frac{1}{\sqrt{\frac{10}{3}}}\sin\sqrt{\frac{10}{3}}t$$

$$\implies \quad L^{-1}\frac{s-2}{6s^2+20} = \frac{1}{6}\cos\sqrt{\frac{10}{3}}t - \frac{1}{\sqrt{30}}\sin\sqrt{\frac{10}{3}}t$$

Example 3 Find the inverse laplace transform of $\frac{3s}{2s+9}$.
Sol. Since we have $L^{-1}\frac{3}{2s+9} - \frac{3}{2}L^{-1}\frac{1}{s+9/2} = \frac{3}{2}c^{-9t/2}$.
Now we have

$$L^{-1}\frac{3s}{2s+9} = \frac{3}{2}\frac{d}{dt}e^{-9t/2} + \frac{3}{2}e^{-9.0/2}\delta(t) \qquad \text{[by multiplication by s]}$$

$$\implies \quad L^{-1}\frac{3s}{2s+9} = \frac{3}{2}(-\frac{9}{2})e^{-9t/2} + \frac{3}{2} = -\frac{27}{4}e^{-9t/2} + \frac{3}{2}.$$

Example 4 Find the inverse laplace transform of following functions:
$i.\ \frac{s^2+3}{s(s^2+9)}$ $\quad ii.\ \frac{s+1}{s^2-6s+25}$ $\quad iii.\ \frac{1}{(s+2)^5}$ $\quad iv.\ \frac{e^{-s}}{(s+1)^3}$ $\quad v.\ \frac{e^{-s}-3e^{-3s}}{s^2}$.
Sol. i. Since

$$L^{-1}\frac{s^2+3}{s(s^2+9)} = L^{-1}\frac{s^2+9-6}{s(s^2+9)} = L^{-1}[\frac{1}{s} - \frac{6}{s(s^2+9)}]$$

$$\implies \quad L^{-1}\frac{s^2+3}{s(s^2+9)} = 1 - 2\int_0^t \sin 3t dt \qquad \text{[Division by s property]}$$

$$\implies \quad L^{-1}\frac{s^2+3}{s(s^2+9)} = 1 + \frac{2}{3}[\cos 3t]_0^t = 1 + \frac{2}{3}\cos 3t - \frac{2}{3} = \frac{1}{3}[2\cos 3t + 1]$$

ii. Since

$$L^{-1}\frac{s+1}{s^2-6s+25} = L^{-1}\frac{s+1}{s^2-6s+9+16} = L^{-1}\frac{s-3+4}{(s-3)^2+4^2}$$

$$\Longrightarrow \quad L^{-1}\tfrac{s+1}{s^2-6s+25} = L^{-1}\tfrac{s-3}{(s-3)^2+4^2} + L^{-1}\tfrac{4}{(s-3)^2+4^2}$$

$$\Longrightarrow L^{-1}\tfrac{s+1}{s^2-6s+25} = e^{3t}L^{-1}\tfrac{s}{s^2+4^2} + 4e^{3t}L^{-1}\tfrac{1}{s^2+4^2} \quad \text{[by first shifting property]}$$

$$\Longrightarrow \quad L^{-1}\tfrac{s+1}{s^2-6s+25} = e^{3t}\cos 4t + e^{3t}\sin 4t.$$

iii. Since

$$L^{-1}\tfrac{1}{(s+2)^5} = e^{-2t}L^{-1}\tfrac{1}{s^5} \qquad \text{[by first shifting property]}$$

$$\Longrightarrow \quad L^{-1}\tfrac{1}{(s+2)^5} = e^{-2t}\tfrac{t^4}{4!}$$

iv. Since we know that

$$L^{-1}\tfrac{1}{s^3} = \tfrac{t^2}{2!} \quad \Longrightarrow \quad L^{-1}\tfrac{1}{(s+1)^3} = e^{-t}\tfrac{t^2}{2!}$$

Thus by second shifting property we have

$$L^{-1}\tfrac{e^{-s}}{(s+1)^3} = e^{-(t-1)}\tfrac{(t-1)^2}{2!}u(t-1)$$

v. Since

$$L^{-1}[\frac{e^{-s} - 3e^{-3s}}{s^2}] = L^{-1}[\frac{e^{-s}}{s^2} - \frac{3e^{-3s}}{s^2}] \tag{2.1}$$

Since we know that

$$L[u(t-a)] = \tfrac{e^{-as}}{s}$$

and

$$L[(t-a)u(t-a)] = \tfrac{e^{-as}}{s^2}$$

Using above result in equation (2.1) we have

$$L^{-1}[\tfrac{e^{-s}-3e^{-3s}}{s^2}] = (t-1)u(t-1) - 3(t-3)u(t-3).$$

Example 5 Find the value of $L^{-1}[\frac{1}{(s^2+a^2)^2}]$.
Sol. The given expression can be rewritten as

$$L^{-1}[\tfrac{1}{(s^2+a^2)^2}] = \tfrac{1}{s}\tfrac{s}{(s^2+a^2)^2} = -\tfrac{1}{2s}\tfrac{d}{ds}[\tfrac{1}{(s^2+a^2)}]$$

$$\Longrightarrow \quad = \tfrac{1}{2a}\int_0^{\infty} t\sin at dt \qquad \text{[by derivative and division by s property]}$$

$$\Longrightarrow \quad = \tfrac{1}{2a}[-\tfrac{t}{a}\cos at + \tfrac{\sin at}{a^2}]_0^t = \tfrac{1}{2a^3}[-at\cos at + \sin at].$$

Example 6 Find $L^{-1}[\log\frac{s+1}{s-1}]$.
Sol. By using inverse laplace of the derivative property we have

$$L^{-1}[\log\frac{s+1}{s-1}] = -\frac{1}{t}L^{-1}[\frac{d}{ds}\log\frac{s+1}{s-1}]$$

$$\implies \quad L^{-1}[\log\frac{s+1}{s-1}] = -\frac{1}{t}L^{-1}[\frac{d}{ds}\log(s+1) - \frac{d}{ds}\log(s-1)]$$

$$\implies \quad L^{-1}[\log\frac{s+1}{s-1}] = -\frac{1}{t}L^{-1}[\frac{1}{s+1} - \frac{1}{s-1}] = \frac{1}{t}L^{-1}[e^t - e^{-t}].$$

Example 7 Find the function whose laplace transform is $\log(1+\frac{1}{s})$.
Sol. By using inverse laplace of the derivative property we have

$$L^{-1}[\log(1+\frac{1}{s})] = -\frac{1}{t}L^{-1}[\frac{d}{ds}\log(1+\frac{1}{s})]$$

$$= -\frac{1}{t}L^{-1}[\frac{s}{s+1}(-\frac{1}{s^2})] = -\frac{1}{t}L^{-1}[-\frac{1}{s(s+1)}]$$

$$= -\frac{1}{t}L^{-1}[\frac{1}{(s+1)} - \frac{1}{s}] = -\frac{1}{t}[L^{-1}(\frac{1}{(s+1)}) - L^{-1}(\frac{1}{s})]$$

$$= -\frac{1}{t}[e^{-t} - 1] = \frac{1}{t}[1 - e^{-t}].$$

Example 8 Find the inverse laplace transform of $\tan^{-1}(\frac{2}{s^2})$.
Sol. By using inverse laplace of the derivative property we have

$$L^{-1}[\tan^{-1}(\frac{2}{s^2})] = -\frac{1}{t}L^{-1}[\frac{d}{ds}\tan^{-1}(\frac{2}{s^2})] = -\frac{1}{t}L^{-1}[\frac{1}{1+\frac{4}{s^2}}(-\frac{4}{s^3})]$$

$$= -\frac{1}{t}L^{-1}[\frac{s^4}{s^4+4}(-\frac{4}{s^3})] = \frac{1}{t}L^{-1}[\frac{4s}{s^4+4}] = \frac{4}{t}L^{-1}[\frac{s}{s^4+4}]$$

$$= \frac{4}{t}L^{-1}[\frac{s}{(s^2+2s+2)(s^2-2s+2)}] = \frac{1}{t}L^{-1}[-\frac{1}{s^2+2s+2} + \frac{1}{s^2-2s+2}]$$

$$= \frac{1}{t}L^{-1}[-\frac{1}{(s+1)^2+1} + \frac{1}{(s-1)^2+1}] = \frac{1}{t}[e^{-t}\sin t + e^t\sin t]$$

$$\implies \qquad L^{-1}[\tan^{-1}(\frac{2}{s^2})] = \frac{\sin t}{t}[e^t - e^{-t}].$$

Example 9 Obtain inverse laplace transform of $\cot^{-1}\frac{s+3}{2}$.
Sol. By using inverse laplace of the derivative property we have

$$L^{-1}[\cot^{-1}(\frac{s+3}{2})] = -\frac{1}{t}L^{-1}[\frac{d}{ds}\cot^{-1}(\frac{s+3}{2})]$$

$$= -\frac{1}{t}L^{-1}[\frac{-1/2}{1+(\frac{s+3}{2})^2}] = \frac{1}{2t}L^{-1}[\frac{4}{4+(s+3)^2}]$$

$$= \frac{1}{t} L^{-1}[\frac{2}{2^2+(s+3)^2}] = \frac{1}{t} e^{-3t} L^{-1}[\frac{2}{2^2+s^2}]$$

$$\implies \qquad L^{-1}[\cot^{-1}(\frac{s+3}{2})] = \frac{e^{-3t}}{t} \sin 2t.$$

Example 10 Find the inverse laplace transform of $\frac{s^2-a^2}{(s^2+a^2)^2}$.
Sol. Since we know that

$$L^{-1}[\frac{s}{s^2+a^2}] = \cos at$$

$$\therefore \qquad L^{-1}[\frac{d}{ds}(\frac{s}{s^2+a^2})] = -t \cos at$$

$$\implies \qquad L^{-1}[\frac{a^2-s^2}{(s^2+a^2)^2}] = -t \cos at$$

$$\implies \qquad L^{-1}[\frac{s^2-a^2}{(s^2+a^2)^2}] = t \cos at.$$

Example 11 Find the inverse laplace transform of $\frac{1}{s^4+4}$.
Sol. The given function can be written as

$$\frac{1}{s^4+4} = \frac{1}{4s}[\frac{1}{s^2-2s+2} - \frac{1}{s^2+2s+2}] \qquad \text{[By partial fraction]}$$

Taking laplace transform both side of above equation we have

$$L^{-1}[\frac{1}{s^4+4}] = L^{-1}[\frac{1}{4s}(\frac{1}{s^2-2s+2} - \frac{1}{s^2+2s+2})]$$

$$\implies \qquad L^{-1}[\frac{1}{s^4+4}] = \frac{1}{4}\int_0^t [L^{-1}(\frac{1}{s^2-2s+2} - \frac{1}{s^2+2s+2})]dt \qquad \text{[By integral property]}$$

$$\implies \qquad L^{-1}[\frac{1}{s^4+4}] = \frac{1}{4}\int_0^t [L^{-1}(\frac{1}{(s-1)^2+1} - \frac{1}{(s+1)^2+1})]dt$$

$$\implies \qquad L^{-1}[\frac{1}{s^4+4}] = \frac{1}{4}\int_0^t (e^t \sin t - e^{-t} \sin t)dt \qquad \text{[By first shifting property]}$$

$$\implies \qquad L^{-1}[\frac{1}{s^4+4}] = \frac{1}{4}\int_0^t (e^t - e^{-t}) \sin t dt$$

$$\implies \qquad L^{-1}[\frac{1}{s^4+4}] = \frac{1}{4}[\frac{e^t}{2}(\sin t - \cos t) - \frac{e^{-t}}{2}(-\sin t - \cos t)]$$

$$\implies \qquad L^{-1}[\frac{1}{s^4+4}] = \frac{1}{4}[\sin t(\frac{e^t+e^{-t}}{2}) - \cos t(\frac{e^t-e^{-t}}{2})]$$

$$\implies \qquad L^{-1}[\frac{1}{s^4+4}] = \frac{1}{4}[\sin t \cosh t - \cos t \sinh t].$$

Example 12 Find the inverse laplace transform of $\frac{e^{-2\pi s}}{s(s^2+1)}$.
Sol. Here we have

$$L^{-1}[\frac{e^{-2\pi s}}{s(s^2+1)}] = L^{-1}[\frac{e^{-2\pi s}}{s} - \frac{se^{-2\pi s}}{(s^2+1)}]$$

$$\Longrightarrow L^{-1}[\frac{e^{-2\pi s}}{s(s^2+1)}] = u(t-2\pi) - \cos(t-2\pi)u(t-2\pi) \text{ [By Second shifting property]}$$

where $u(t-2\pi)$ is unit step function.
Example 13 Find the inverse laplace transform of $\frac{5s+3}{(s-1)(s^2+2s+5)}$.
Sol. By using partial fraction method above equation can be written as

$$\frac{5s+3}{(s-1)(s^2+2s+5)} = \frac{1}{s-1} - \frac{s-2}{s^2+2s+5}$$

Taking laplace inverse of above equation we have

$$L^{-1}\frac{5s+3}{(s-1)(s^2+2s+5)} = L^{-1}\frac{1}{s-1} - L^{-1}\frac{s-2}{s^2+2s+5}$$

$$= L^{-1}\frac{1}{s-1} - L^{-1}\frac{s+1}{(s+1)^2+2^2} + L^{-1}\frac{3}{(s+1)^2+2^2}$$

$$= e^t - e^{-t}L^{-1}\frac{s}{s^2+2^2} + 3e^{-t}L^{-1}\frac{1}{s^2+2^2}$$

Thus

$$L^{-1}\frac{5s+3}{(s-1)(s^2+2s+5)} = e^t - e^{-t}\cos 2t + \frac{3}{2}e^{-t}\sin 2t$$

Example 14 Use convolution theorem to evaluate $L^{-1}[\frac{s}{(s^2+4)^2}]$.
Sol. The given equation can be written as

$$\frac{s}{(s^2+4)^2} = \frac{1}{s^2+4}.\frac{s}{s^2+4}$$

Now let $F(s) = \frac{1}{s^2+4}$ and $G(s) = \frac{s}{s^2+4}$. Then $L^{-1}F(s) = L^{-1}\frac{1}{s^2+4} = \frac{1}{2}\sin 2t = f(t)$ and $L^{-1}G(s) = L^{-1}\frac{s}{s^2+4} = \cos 2t = g(t)$.
Now by convolution theorem we have

$$L^{-1}[F(s).G(s)] = \int_0^t f(x)g(t-x)dx = \frac{1}{2}\int_0^t \sin 2x \cos 2(t-x)dx$$

$$= \frac{1}{4}\int_0^t [\sin 2t + \sin(4x-2t)]dx$$

$$= \frac{1}{4}[x\sin 2t - \frac{1}{4}\cos(4x-2t)]_0^t$$

$$= \frac{1}{4}[t \sin 2t - \frac{1}{4}\cos(4t - 2t) + \frac{1}{4}\cos(-2t)]$$

$$\Longrightarrow \quad L^{-1}[F(s).G(s)] = L^{-1}[\frac{s}{(s^2+4)^2}] = \frac{1}{4}\sin 2t.$$

Example 15 Use convolution theorem to find inverse of the function $\frac{1}{(s^2+a^2)^2}$.
Sol. The given equation can be written as

$$\frac{1}{(s^2+a^2)^2} = \frac{1}{s^2+a^2}\cdot\frac{1}{s^2+a^2}$$

Now let $F(s) = \frac{1}{s^2+a^2}$ and $G(s) = \frac{s}{s^2+a^2}$. Then $L^{-1}F(s) = L^{-1}\frac{1}{s^2+a^2} = \frac{1}{a}\sin at = f(t)$ and $L^{-1}G(s) = L^{-1}\frac{1}{s^2+a^2} = \frac{1}{a}\sin at = g(t)$.
Now by convolution theorem we have

$$L^{-1}[F(s).G(s)] = \int_0^t f(x)g(t-x)dx = \frac{1}{a^2}\int_0^t \sin ax \sin a(t-x)dx$$

$$= \frac{1}{2a^2}\int_0^t [\cos(2ax - at) - \cos at]dx$$

$$= \frac{1}{2a^2}[\frac{1}{2a}\sin(2ax - at) - x\cos at]_0^t$$

$$= \frac{1}{2a^2}[\frac{1}{2a}\sin at - t\cos at + \frac{1}{2a}\sin at]$$

$$\Longrightarrow \quad L^{-1}[F(s).G(s)] = L^{-1}\frac{1}{(s^2+a^2)^2} = \frac{1}{2a^3}[\sin at - at\cos at].$$

Example 16 Use convolution theorem to find $L^{-1}[\frac{s^2}{(s^2+a^2)(s^2+b^2)}], \ a \neq b$.
Sol. The given equation can be written as

$$\frac{s^2}{(s^2+a^2)(s^2+b^2)} = \frac{s}{s^2+a^2}\cdot\frac{s}{s^2+b^2}$$

Now let $F(s) = \frac{s}{s^2+a^2}$ and $G(s) = \frac{s}{s^2+b^2}$. Then $L^{-1}F(s) = L^{-1}\frac{s}{s^2+a^2} = \cos at = f(t)$ and $L^{-1}G(s) = L^{-1}\frac{s}{s^2+b^2} = \cos bt = g(t)$.
Now by convolution theorem we have

$$L^{-1}[F(s).G(s)] = \int_0^t f(x)g(t-x)dx = \int_0^t \cos ax \cos b(t-x)dx$$

$$= \frac{1}{2}\int_0^t (\cos[(a-b)x + bt] + \cos[(a+b)x - bt])dx$$

$$= \frac{1}{2}[\frac{\sin[(a-b)x+bt]}{a-b} + \frac{\sin[(a+b)x-bt]}{a+b}]_0^t$$

$$= \frac{1}{2}[\frac{\sin at - \sin bt}{a-b} + \frac{\sin at + \sin bt}{a+b}]$$

Thus

$$L^{-1}[F(s).G(s)] = L^{-1}[\frac{s^2}{(s^2+a^2)(s^2+b^2)}] = \frac{a\sin at - b\sin bt}{a^2-b^2}.$$

Example 17 Using convolution theorem, prove that

$$L^{-1}[\frac{1}{s^3(s^2+1)}] = \frac{t^2}{2} + \cos t - 1.$$

Sol. The given equation can be written as

$$\frac{1}{s^3(s^2+1)} = \frac{1}{s^3}.\frac{1}{s^2+1}$$

Now let $F(s) = \frac{1}{s^2+1}$ and $G(s) = \frac{1}{s^3}$. Then $L^{-1}F(s) = L^{-1}\frac{1}{s^2+1} = \sin t = f(t)$ and $L^{-1}G(s) = L^{-1}\frac{1}{s^3} = \frac{t^2}{2!} = g(t)$.
Now by convolution theorem we have

$$L^{-1}[F(s).G(s)] = \int_0^t f(x)g(t-x)dx = \int_0^t \sin x.\frac{(t-x)^2}{2!}dx$$

$$= \frac{1}{2}\int_0^t (t^2 + x^2 - 2tx)\sin x dx$$

$$= \frac{1}{2}[(t^2 + x^2 - 2tx)(-\cos x) + 2\int(x-t)\cos x dx]_0^t$$

$$= \frac{1}{2}[(t^2 + x^2 - 2tx)(-\cos x) + 2(x-t)\sin x + 2\cos x]_0^t$$

$$= \frac{1}{2}[2\cos t + t^2 - 2]$$

Thus

$$L^{-1}[F(s).G(s)] = L^{-1}[\frac{1}{s^3(s^2+1)}] = \frac{t^2}{2} + \cos t - 1.$$

Heaviside inverse formula of $\frac{F(s)}{G(s)}$

If $F(s)$ and $G(s)$ be two polynomial in S and the degree of $F(s)$ is less than that of $G(s)$. Further if $\alpha_1, \alpha_2, \alpha_3, ...\alpha_n$ be n roots of the equation $G(s) = 0$ then the inverse laplace formula of $\frac{F(s)}{G(s)}$ is given by

$$L^{-1}\frac{F(s)}{G(s)} = \sum_{i=1}^{n}\frac{F(\alpha_i)}{G'(\alpha_i)}e^{\alpha_i t}.$$

the above formula is known as Heaviside inverse formula for inverse laplace transform of $\frac{F(s)}{G(s)}$.

Example 18 Find $L^{-1}[\frac{2s^2-6s+5}{s^3-6s^2+11s-6}]$ by using Heaviside inverse formula.
Sol. Let $F(s) = 2s^2-6s+5$ and $G(s) = s^3-6s^2+11s-6 = (s-1)(s-2)(s-3)$.
Further the roots of $G(s) = 0$ are 1, 2, 3.
So we again let $\alpha_1 = 1, \alpha_2 = 2, \alpha_3 = 3$ and $G'(s) = 3s^2 - 12s + 11$.
Now from Heaviside inverse formula we have

$$L^{-1}\frac{F(s)}{G(s)} = \sum_{i=1}^{n} \frac{F(\alpha_i)}{G'(\alpha_i)} e^{\alpha_i t}$$

$$L^{-1}[\frac{2s^2-6s+5}{s^3-6s^2+11s-6}] = \frac{F(\alpha_1)}{G'(\alpha_1)} e^{\alpha_1 t} + \frac{F(\alpha_2)}{G'(\alpha_2)} e^{\alpha_2 t} + \frac{F(\alpha_3)}{G'(\alpha_3)} e^{\alpha_3 t}$$

$$L^{-1}[\frac{2s^2-6s+5}{s^3-6s^2+11s-6}] = \frac{F(1)}{G'(1)} e^{t} + \frac{F(2)}{G'(2)} e^{2t} + \frac{F(3)}{G'(3)} e^{3t}$$

Thus we have

$$L^{-1}[\frac{2s^2-6s+5}{s^3-6s^2+11s-6}] = \frac{1}{2}e^{t} - e^{2t} + \frac{5}{2}e^{3t}$$

2.4 Miscellaneous Exercise

1. Find inverse laplace transform of following functions:
i. $\frac{2s-5}{9s^2-25}$ *ii.* $\frac{1}{4s} + \frac{16}{1-s^2}$ *iii.* $\frac{s}{2s^2-1}$ *iv.* $\frac{s^2+4}{s^2+9}$
Ans. *i.* $\frac{2}{9}\cosh\frac{5t}{3} - \frac{1}{3}\sin\frac{5t}{3}$ *ii.* $\frac{1}{4} - 16\sinh t$ *iii.* $\frac{1}{2}\cosh\frac{t}{2}$ *iv.* $-\frac{5}{3}\sin 3t + 1$.
2.Find inverse laplace transform of following functions:
i. $\frac{1}{2s(s-3)}$ *ii.* $\frac{s^2+2}{s(s^2+4)}$ *iii.* $\frac{1}{s^3(s^2+1)}$ *iv.* $\frac{s}{s^2+6s+25}$
Ans. *i.* $\frac{1}{2}[\frac{e^{3t}}{3} - 1]$ *ii.* $\cos^2 t$ *iii.* $\frac{t^2}{2} + \cos t - 1$ *iv.* $e^{-3t}[\cos 4t - \frac{3}{4}\sin 4t]$.
3.Find inverse laplace transform of following functions:
i. $\frac{s}{(s+7)^4}$ *ii.* $\frac{1}{2(s-1)^2+32}$ *iii.* $\frac{e^{-s}}{\sqrt{s+1}}$ *iv.* $\frac{e^{-\pi s}}{s^2+1}$
Ans. *i.* $\frac{t^2}{6}e^{-7t}(3-7t)$ *ii.* $\frac{e^t}{8}\sin 4t$ *iii.* $\frac{e^{-(t-1)}}{\sqrt{\pi(t-1)}}u(t-1)$ *iv.* $-\sin t.u(t-\pi)$.
4. Find the inverse laplace transform of $\cot^{-1}\frac{s}{2}$.
Ans. $\frac{1}{t}\sin 2t$.
5. Find the inverse laplace transform of $\frac{s+1}{(s^2+6s+13)^2}$.
Ans. $\frac{e^{-3t}}{8}[2t.\sin 2t - \sin 2t + 2t\cos 2t]$.
6. Find the inverse laplace transform of $\frac{s}{1+s^2+s^4}$.
Ans. $\frac{2}{\sqrt{3}}\sin\frac{\sqrt{3}}{2}t\sinh\frac{t}{2}$.
7. Find the inverse laplace transform of $\frac{1}{2}\log\frac{s^2+b^2}{(s-a)^2}$.
Ans. $\frac{e^{-at}-\cos bt}{t}$.
8. Find the inverse laplace transform of $\frac{s^3}{s^4-a^4}$.
Ans. $\frac{1}{2}(\cosh at + \cos at)$.
9. Find the inverse laplace transform of $\frac{s+4}{s(s-1)(s^2+4)}$.
Ans. $-1 + e^t - \frac{1}{2}\sin 2t$.
10. Find the inverse laplace transform of $\frac{11s^2-2s+5}{2s^3-3s^2-3s+2}$.

Ans. $2e^{-t} + 5e^{2t} - \frac{3}{2}e^{t/2}$.
11. Find the inverse laplace transform of $\frac{16}{(s^2+2s+5)^2}$.
Ans. $e^{-t}(\sin 2t - 2t\cos 2t)$.
12. Find the inverse laplace transform of $\frac{s^2-6s+7}{(s^2-4s+5)^2}$.
Ans. $te^{2t}(\cos t - \sin t)$.
13. Find inverse laplace transform by convolution theorem of $\frac{1}{(s+2)^2(s-2)}$.
Ans. $\frac{e^{2t}}{16} - \frac{e^{-2t}}{16}(4t+1)$.
14. Find inverse laplace transform by convolution theorem of $\frac{s}{(s^2+a^2)^2}$.
Ans. $\frac{t\sin at}{2a}$.
15. Find inverse laplace transform by convolution theorem of $\frac{1}{s^2(s^2-a^2)}$.
Ans. $\frac{1}{a^3}(-at + \sinh at)$.
16. Find inverse laplace transform by convolution theorem of $\frac{s}{(s^2+1)(s^2+4)}$.
Ans. $\frac{1}{3}(\cos t - \cos 2t)$.
17. Find inverse laplace transform by Heaviside expansion formula of $\frac{2s+3}{(s-2)(s-3)(s-4)}$.
Ans. $\frac{7}{2}e^{2t} - 9e^{3t} + \frac{11}{2}e^{4t}$.
18. Find inverse laplace transform by Heaviside expansion formula of $\frac{s-1}{s^2+3s+2}$.
Ans. $-2e^{-t} + 3e^{-2t}$.
18. Find inverse laplace transform by Heaviside expansion formula of $\frac{2s^2+5s-4}{s^3+s^2-2s}$.
Ans. $2 + e^t - e^{-2t}$.
19. Find inverse laplace transform by Heaviside expansion formula of $\frac{11s^2-2s+5}{2s^3-3s^2-3s+2}$.
Ans. $2e^{-t} + 5e^{2t} - \frac{3}{2}e^{t/2}$.
20. Find inverse laplace transform by convolution theorem of $\frac{1}{(s^2+1)^3}$.
Ans. $\frac{1}{8}[(3-t^2)\sin t - 3t\cos t]$.
20. Find inverse laplace transform by convolution theorem of $\frac{3s+1}{(s-1)(s^2+1)}$.
Ans. $e^t - 2\cos t + \sin t$.

Chapter 3

Applications of Laplace transform

Ordinary linear differential equations with constant coefficients can be easily solved using the Laplace transform method, without the need to find the general solution or arbitrary constants. The method will be illustrated through the following examples:

3.1 Solved Problems

Example 1 Solve the ordinary differential equation by laplace transform

$$\frac{d^3}{dt^3} + 2\frac{d^2}{dt^2} - \frac{dy}{dt} - 2y = 0, \quad \text{where} \quad y = 1, \frac{dy}{dt} = 2, \frac{d^2}{dt^2} = 2 \text{ at } t = 0.$$

Sol. The given equation can be written as

$$y^{'''} + 2y^{''} - y^{'} - 2y = 0 \tag{3.1}$$

Taking laplace transform of both sides of equation (3.1) we have

$$L[y^{'''}] + 2L[y^{''}] - L[y^{'}] - 2L[y] = 0$$

By using laplace transform of derivative of a function property we have

$$[s^3\bar{y} - s^2y(0) - sy^{'}(0) - y^{''}(0)] + 2[s^2\bar{y} - sy(0) - y^{'}(0)] - [s\bar{y} - y(0)] - 2\bar{y} = 0$$

where $\bar{y} = L[y]$.
Now using given initial condition in above equation we have

$$(s^3 + 2s^2 - s - 2)\bar{y} = s^2 + 4s + 5$$

$$\implies \quad \bar{y} = \frac{s^2+4s+5}{s^3+2s^2-s-2} = \frac{s^2+4s+5}{(s-1)(s+1)(s+2)}$$

$$\implies \quad \bar{y} = \frac{5}{s(s-1)} - \frac{1}{s+1} + \frac{1}{3(s+2)} \qquad \text{[By partial fraction]}$$

Taking inverse laplace transform of above equation we have

$$L^{-1}[\bar{y}] = y = \frac{5}{3}L^{-1}(\frac{1}{s-1}) - L^{-1}(\frac{1}{s+1}) + \frac{1}{3}L^{-1}(\frac{1}{s+2})$$

$$y = \frac{5}{3}e^t - e^{-t} + \frac{1}{3}e^{-2t}.$$

Example 2 Solve the following equation by laplace transform

$$y^{'''} - 2y^{''} + 5y^{'} = 0, \qquad y = 0, y^{'} = 1 \text{ at } t = 0 \text{ and } y = 1 \text{ at } t = \pi/8.$$

Sol. Taking laplace transform of both sides of given equation we have

$$L[y^{'''}] - 2L[y^{''}] + 5L[y^{'}] = L[0]$$

By using laplace transform of derivative of a function property we have

$$[s^3\bar{y} - s^2y(0) - sy^{'}(0) - y^{''}(0)] - 2[s^2\bar{y} - sy(0) - y^{'}(0)] + 5[s\bar{y} - y(0)] = 0$$

where $\bar{y} = L[y]$.
Now using given initial condition in above equation we have

$$(s^3 - 2s^2 + 5s)\bar{y} - s - k + 2 = 0 \qquad [\text{Let } y^{''}(0) = k]$$

$$\implies \quad \bar{y} = \frac{(k-2)+s}{s(s^2-2s+5)} = (\frac{k-2}{5})(\frac{1}{s} - \frac{s-2}{s^2-2s+5}) + \frac{1}{s^2-2s+5}$$

$$\implies \quad \bar{y} = (\frac{k-2}{5})(\frac{1}{s}) - (\frac{k-2}{5})[\frac{s-1}{(s-1)^2+4}] + (\frac{k+3}{10})[\frac{1}{(s-1)^2+4}]$$

Taking inverse laplace transform on both side of above equation we have

$$L^{-1}\bar{y} = y = (\frac{k-2}{5}) - (\frac{k-2}{5})e^t\cos 2t + (\frac{k+3}{10})e^t\sin 2t \qquad (3.2)$$

Now putting $y(\pi/8) = 1$ in above equation we get $k = 7$.
Now putting the value of k in equation (3.2) we have

$$y = 1 + e^t(\sin 2t - \cos 2t).$$

Example 3 Using laplace transform, find the solution of the initial value problem

$$y^{''} + 9y = 6\cos 3t \qquad y(0) = 2, \;\; y^{'}(0) = 0.$$

Sol. Taking laplace transform of both sides of given equation we have

$$L[y^{''}] + 9L[y] = 6L[\cos 3t]$$

By using laplace transform of derivative of a function property we have

$$[s^2\bar{y} - sy(0) - y^{'}(0)] + 9\bar{y} = 6\tfrac{s}{s^2+9}$$

where $\bar{y} = L[y]$.
Now using given initial condition in above equation we have

$$s^2\bar{y} - 2s + 9\bar{y} = \tfrac{6s}{s^2+9}$$

$$\Longrightarrow \qquad (s^2+9)\bar{y} = 2s + \tfrac{6s}{s^2+9}$$

$$\Longrightarrow \qquad \bar{y} = \tfrac{2s}{s^2+9} + \tfrac{6s}{(s^2+9)^2}$$

Taking inverse laplace transform of above equation we have

$$L^{-1}\bar{y} = y = L^{-1}\tfrac{2s}{s^2+9} + L^{-1}\tfrac{6s}{(s^2+9)^2}$$

$$\Longrightarrow \qquad y = 2\cos 3t + L^{-1}[\tfrac{d}{ds}(\tfrac{-3}{s^2+9})] = 2\cos 3t - t\sin 3t.$$

Example 4 Using laplace transform sole the following differential equation:

$$\tfrac{d^2x}{dt^2} + 9x = \cos 2t \quad \text{if} \quad x(0) = 1, \quad x(\pi/2) = -1.$$

Sol. Taking laplace transform of both sides of given equation we have

$$L[x^{''}] + 9L[x] = 6L[\cos 2t]$$

By using laplace transform of derivative of a function property we have

$$[s^2\bar{x} - sx(0) - x^{'}(0)] + 9\bar{x} = \tfrac{s}{s^2+4}$$

where $\bar{x} = L[x]$.
Now using given initial condition in above equation we have

$$(s^2+9)\bar{x} = s + \tfrac{s}{s^2+4} + k \qquad [\text{Let } k = x^{'}(0)]$$

$$\implies \qquad \bar{x} = \tfrac{1}{5}\tfrac{s}{s^2+4} + \tfrac{4}{5}\tfrac{s}{s^2+9} + \tfrac{k}{s^2+9}$$

Taking inverse laplace transform of above equation we have

$$L^{-1}(\bar{x}) = x = L^{-1}(\tfrac{1}{5}\tfrac{s}{s^2+4}) + L^{-1}(\tfrac{4}{5}\tfrac{s}{s^2+9}) + L^{-1}(\tfrac{k}{s^2+9})$$

$$\implies \qquad x = \frac{1}{5}\cos 2t + \frac{4}{5}\cos 3t + \frac{1}{3}k\sin 3t \tag{3.3}$$

Now putting $x(\pi/2) = -1$ in equation (3.3) we get $k = 12/5$.
Now using $k = 12/5$ in equation (3.3) we have

$$x = \tfrac{1}{5}[\cos 2t + 4\cos 3t + 4\sin 3t].$$

Example 5 Solve initial value problem by using laplace transform $y'' + 4y' + 4y = 6e^{-t}$, with initial conditions $y(0) = -2$ and $y'(0) = 8$.
Sol. Taking laplace transform of both sides of given equation we have

$$L[y''] + 4L[y'] + 4L[y] = 6L[e^{-t}]$$

By using laplace transform of derivative of a function property we have

$$[s^2\bar{y} - sy(0) - y'(0)] + 4[s\bar{y} - y(0)] + 4\bar{y} = \tfrac{6}{s+1}$$

where $\bar{y} = L[y]$.
Now using given initial condition in above equation we have

$$(s+2)^2\bar{y} = \tfrac{6}{s+1} - 2s$$

$$\implies \qquad \bar{y} = \tfrac{6}{(s+1)(s+2)^2} - \tfrac{2s}{(s+2)^2}$$

$$\implies \qquad \bar{y} = \tfrac{6}{(s+1)} - \tfrac{8}{s+2} - \tfrac{2}{(s+2)^2} \qquad \text{[By partial fraction]}$$

Taking inverse laplace transform of above equation we have

$$L^{-1}\bar{y} = y = L^{-1}(\tfrac{6}{(s+1)}) - L^{-1}(\tfrac{8}{s+2}) - L^{-1}(\tfrac{2}{(s+2)^2})$$

$$\implies \qquad y = 6e^{-t} - 8e^{-2t} - 2te^{-2t}.$$

Example 6 Solve the following differential equation using laplace transform
$\frac{d^3y}{dt^3} - 3\frac{d^2y}{dt^2} + 3\frac{dy}{dt} - y = t^2e^t$ where $y(0) = 1,\ (dy/dt)_{t=0} = 0, (\frac{d^2y}{dt^2})_{t=0} = -2$

Sol. Taking laplace transform of both sides of given equation we have

$$L[y'''] - 3L[y''] + 3L[y'] - L[y] = L[t^2e^t]$$

By using laplace transform of derivative of a function property we have

$$[s^3\bar{y} - s^2y(0) - sy'(0) - y''(0)] - [s^2\bar{y} - sy(0) - y'(0)] + 3[s\bar{y} - y(0)] - \bar{y} = \frac{2}{(s-1)^3}$$

where $\bar{y} = L[y]$.
Now using given initial condition in above equation we have

$$(s^3 - 3s^2 + 3s - 1)\bar{y} = \frac{2}{(s-1)^3} + s^2 - 3s + 1$$

$$\implies \quad (s-1)^3\bar{y} = \frac{2}{(s-1)^3} + s^2 - 3s + 1$$

$$\implies \quad \bar{y} = \frac{s^2-3s+1}{(s-1)^3} + \frac{2}{(s-1)^6}$$

$$\implies \quad \bar{y} = \frac{1}{s-1} - \frac{1}{(s-1)^2} - \frac{1}{(s-1)^3} + \frac{2}{(s-1)^6} \qquad \text{[By partial fractions]}$$

Taking inverse laplace transform of above equation we have

$$L^{-1}\bar{y} = y = L^{-1}\frac{1}{s-1} - L^{-1}\frac{1}{(s-1)^2} - L^{-1}\frac{1}{(s-1)^3} + L^{-1}\frac{2}{(s-1)^6}$$

Thus

$$\implies \quad y = e^t(1 - t - \frac{t^2}{t} + \frac{t^5}{60})$$

Example 7 Solve $\frac{d^2y}{dx^2} + 2\frac{dy}{dx} + 5y = e^{-x}\sin x$ where $y(0) = 0, \ \ y'(0) = 1$.
Sol. Taking laplace transform of both sides of given equation we have

$$L[y''] + 2L[y'] + 5L[y] = L[e^{-x}\sin x]$$

By using laplace transform of derivative of a function property we have

$$[s^2\bar{y} - sy(0) - y'(0)] + 2[s\bar{y} - y(0)] + 5\bar{y} = \frac{1}{(s+1)^2+1}$$

where $\bar{y} = L[y]$.
Now using given initial condition in above equation we have

$$(s^2 + 2s + 5)\bar{y} = \frac{s^2+2s+3}{s^2+2s+2} \quad \implies \quad \bar{y} = \frac{s^2+2s+3}{(s^2+2s+5)(s^2+2s+2)}$$

Using partial fraction method we have

$$\bar{y} = \frac{2}{3}\frac{1}{(s^2+2s+5)} + \frac{1}{3}\frac{1}{(s^2+2s+2)}$$

Taking inverse laplace transform we have

$$L^{-1}\bar{y} = y = \tfrac{2}{3}L^{-1}[\tfrac{1}{(s^2+2s+5)}] + \tfrac{1}{3}L^{-1}[\tfrac{1}{(s^2+2s+2)}]$$

$$\implies \qquad y = \tfrac{1}{3}L^{-1}[\tfrac{2}{(s+1)^2+2^2}] + \tfrac{1}{3}L^{-1}[\tfrac{1}{(s+1)^2+1}]$$

$$\implies \qquad y = \tfrac{1}{3}e^{-x}L^{-1}[\tfrac{2}{(s^2+2^2)}] + \tfrac{1}{3}e^{-x}L^{-1}[\tfrac{1}{s^2+1}] \quad \text{[first shifting theorem]}$$

$$\implies \qquad y = \tfrac{1}{3}e^{-x}\sin 2x + \tfrac{1}{3}e^{-x}\sin x$$

Thus

$$y = \tfrac{1}{3}e^{-x}(\sin x + \sin 2x)$$

Example 8 Solve the equation by laplace transform method:

$$\tfrac{dy}{dt} + 2y + \textstyle\int_0^t y\,dt = \sin t, \qquad y(0) = 1.$$

Sol. Taking laplace transform of above equation we have

$$L[\tfrac{dy}{dt}] + 2L[y] + L[\textstyle\int_0^t y\,dt] = L[\sin t]$$

$$[s\bar{y} - y(0)] + 2y + \tfrac{\bar{y}}{s} = \tfrac{1}{s^2+1}$$

Using given initial condition in above equation, we have

$$\bar{y}(s + 2 + \tfrac{1}{s}) = 1 + \tfrac{1}{s^2+1}$$

$$\implies \qquad \bar{y} = \tfrac{s^3+2s}{(s+1)^2(s^2+1)} = \tfrac{1}{s+1} - \tfrac{3}{2}\tfrac{1}{(s+1)^2} + \tfrac{1}{2(s^2+1)} \qquad \text{[By partial fraction]}$$

Taking inverse laplace transform of above equation we have

$$L^{-1}\bar{y} = y = L^{-1}\tfrac{1}{s+1} - \tfrac{3}{2}L^{-1}\tfrac{1}{(s+1)^2} + L^{-1}\tfrac{1}{2(s^2+1)}$$

Thus

$$\implies \qquad y = e^{-t} - \tfrac{3}{2}te^{-t} + \tfrac{1}{2}\sin t$$

Example 9 Solve the differential equation by using laplace transform

$$(D^2 + n^2)x = a\sin(nt + \alpha), \qquad x = Dx = 0 \qquad \text{at } t = 0.$$

Sol. Taking laplace transform of above equation we have

$$[s^2\bar{x} - sx(0) - x^{'}(0)] + n^2\bar{x} = aL[\sin(nt+\alpha)]$$

where $L[x] = \bar{x}$.

$[s^2\bar{x} - sx(0) - x^{'}(0)] + n^2\bar{x} = aL[\sin nt \cos\alpha + \cos nt \sin\alpha] = \frac{a[n\cos\alpha + s\sin\alpha]}{s^2+n^2}$

Using given initial conditions in above equation, we have

$$\bar{x} = a\cos\alpha.\tfrac{n}{(s^2+n^2)^2} + a\sin\alpha.\tfrac{s}{(s^2+n^2)^2}$$

taking inverse laplace transform of above equation we have

$$L^{-1}\bar{x} = x = a\cos\alpha.L^{-1}\frac{n}{(s^2+n^2)^2} + a\sin\alpha.L^{-1}\frac{s}{(s^2+n^2)^2} \tag{3.4}$$

Let us consider second term R. H. S. of equation (3.4)

$L^{-1}\frac{2s}{(s^2+n^2)^2} = L^{-1}\frac{d}{ds}\frac{1}{s^2+n^2} = \frac{t}{n}\sin nt$ [derivative propety of inverse laplace transform]

$$L^{-1}\tfrac{s}{(s^2+n^2)^2} = \tfrac{t}{2n}\sin nt$$

Again

$$L^{-1}\tfrac{1}{s}\tfrac{s}{(s^2+n^2)^2} = \tfrac{1}{2n}\int_0^t t\sin nt dt$$

$$L^{-1}\tfrac{1}{(s^2+n^2)^2} = \tfrac{1}{2n}[t\tfrac{-\cos nt}{n} + \tfrac{1}{n^2}\sin nt]_0^t$$

Thus

$$L^{-1}\tfrac{n}{(s^2+n^2)^2} = \tfrac{1}{2n^2}[-nt\cos nt + \sin nt]$$

Now using the value of $L^{-1}\frac{n}{(s^2+n^2)^2}$ and $L^{-1}\frac{s}{(s^2+n^2)^2}$ in equation (3.4) we have

$$x = a\cos\alpha\tfrac{1}{2n^2}[\sin nt - nt\cos nt] + a\sin\alpha\tfrac{t}{2n}\sin nt$$

$$\implies \quad x = \tfrac{a}{2n^2}[\cos\alpha\sin nt - nt(\cos nt\cos\alpha - \sin nt\sin\alpha)]$$

$$\implies \quad x = \tfrac{a}{2n^2}[\sin nt\cos\alpha - nt\cos(nt+\alpha)].$$

Example 10 Solve $[tD^2 + (1-2t)D - 2]y = 0$, where $y(0) = 1$, $y^{'}(0) = 2$ by using laplace transform.

Sol. Taking laplace transform of given differential equation, we get

$$L[ty''] + L[y'] - 2L[ty'] - 2L[y] = 0$$

$$\implies \quad -\tfrac{d}{ds}L[y''] + L[y'] + 2\tfrac{d}{ds}L[y'] - 2L[y] = 0$$

$$\implies \quad -\tfrac{d}{ds}[s^2\bar{y} - sy(0) - y'(0)] + [s\bar{y} - y(0)] + 2\tfrac{d}{ds}[s\bar{y} - y(0)] - 2\bar{y} = 0$$

where $L[y] = \bar{y}$.
Putting the values of $y(0)$ and $y'(0)$, we get

$$-\tfrac{d}{ds}(s^2\bar{y} - s - 2) + (s\bar{y} - 1) + 2\tfrac{d}{ds}(s\bar{y} - 1) - 2\bar{y} = 0 \quad [\because\ y(0) = 1, y'(0) = 2]$$

$$\implies \quad -s^2\tfrac{d\bar{y}}{ds} - 2s\bar{y} + 1 + s\bar{y} - 1 + 2(s\tfrac{d\bar{y}}{ds} + \bar{y}) - 2\bar{y} = 0$$

$$\implies \quad -(s^2 - 2s)\tfrac{d\bar{y}}{ds} - s\bar{y} = 0$$

$$\implies \quad \tfrac{d\bar{y}}{\bar{y}} - \tfrac{1}{s-2}ds = 0 \quad \text{[By separating the variables]}$$

$$\implies \quad \textstyle\int \tfrac{d\bar{y}}{\bar{y}} + \int \tfrac{1}{s-2}ds = 0 \quad \implies \quad \log\bar{y} + \log(s-2) = \log c$$

$$\implies \quad \log\bar{y}(s-2) = \log c \quad \implies \quad \bar{y}(s-2) = c$$

$$\implies \quad \bar{y} = \tfrac{c}{s-2}$$

Taking inverse laplace transform of above equation we get

$$L^{-1}\bar{y} = cL^{-1}\tfrac{1}{s-2}, \qquad y = ce^{2t}$$

Now putting $y(0) = 1$ in above equation we have

$$1 = ce^0, \qquad \implies c = 1.$$

Using this value of c in the solution we have

$$y = e^{2t}.$$

Example 11 Solve the following simultaneous differential equations by laplace transform

$3\frac{dx}{dt} - y = 2t$, $\frac{dx}{dt} + \frac{dy}{dt} - y = 0$, with the conditions $x(0) = y(0) = 0$.

Sol. Here we have

$$3\frac{dx}{dt} - y = 2t \tag{3.5}$$

and

$$\frac{dx}{dt} + \frac{dy}{dt} - y = 0 \tag{3.6}$$

Taking laplace transform on both sides of equation (3.5) we get

$$3L[x^{'}] - L[y] = L[2t]$$

$$\Longrightarrow \quad 3[s\bar{x} - x(0)] - \bar{y} = \tfrac{2}{s^2}$$

where $L[x] = \bar{x}$ and $L[y] = \bar{y}$.
Using given initial condition we have

$$\Longrightarrow \quad 3s\bar{x} - \bar{y} = \frac{2}{s^2} \tag{3.7}$$

Again taking laplace transform of equation (3.6) we have

$$L[x^{'}] + L[y^{'}] - L[y] = L[0]$$

$$\Longrightarrow \quad [s\bar{x} - x(0)] + [s\bar{y} - y(0)] - \bar{y} = 0$$

Using given initial condition we have

$$s\bar{x} + (s-1)\bar{y} = 0 \tag{3.8}$$

Now solving equation (3.7) and (3.8) we get

$$\bar{x} = \frac{1}{s^3} + \frac{1}{2s^2} - \frac{3}{2s(s-2/3)} \tag{3.9}$$

and

$$\bar{y} = -\frac{2}{s^2(3s-2)} = \frac{1}{s^2} + \frac{3}{2s} - \frac{3}{2(s-2/3)} \tag{3.10}$$

Now taking inverse laplace transform of equation (3.10) we have

$$L^{-1}\bar{y} = y = L^{-1}\tfrac{1}{s^2} + L^{-1}\tfrac{3}{2s} - L^{-1}\tfrac{3}{2(s-2/3)}$$

$$\Longrightarrow \quad y = t + \frac{3}{2} - \frac{3}{2}e^{2t/3} \tag{3.11}$$

Again equation (3.9) can be written as

$$\bar{x} = \tfrac{1}{s^3} + \tfrac{1}{2s^2} - \tfrac{3}{4}[\tfrac{1}{(s-2/3)} - \tfrac{1}{s}]$$

Now taking inverse laplace transform of above equation we have

$$L^{-1}\bar{x} = L^{-1}\tfrac{1}{s^3} + L^{-1}\tfrac{1}{2s^2} - \tfrac{3}{4}[L^{-1}\tfrac{1}{(s-2/3)} - L^{-1}\tfrac{1}{s}]$$

$$\Longrightarrow \qquad x = \frac{t^2}{2} + \frac{t}{2} - \frac{3}{4}e^{2t/3} + \frac{3}{4} \tag{3.12}$$

Thus equation (3.11) and (3.12) when taken together, gives the complete solution.

Example 12 The coordinates (x, y) of a particle moving along a plane curve at ant time t are given by

$$\tfrac{dy}{dt} + 2x = \sin 2t, \text{ and } \tfrac{dx}{dt} - 2y = \cos 2t \qquad (t > 0)$$

It is given that at $t = 0, x = 1$ and $y = 0$. Show by using transforms that the particle moves along the curve $4x^2 + 4xy + 5y^2 = 4$.

Sol. The given equation can be written as

$$2x + Dy = \sin 2t \tag{3.13}$$

and

$$Dx - 2y = \cos 2t \tag{3.14}$$

Where D represents derivative.

Now taking laplace transform of equation (3.13) and using inition condition we have

$$2\bar{x} + s\bar{y} = \frac{2}{s^2 + 4} \tag{3.15}$$

Again taking laplace transform of equation (3.14) and using inition condition we have

$$s\bar{x} - 2\bar{y} = \frac{s}{s^2 + 4} + 1 \tag{3.16}$$

Solving equations (3.15) and (3.16) we get

$$\bar{x} = \frac{1 + s}{4 + s^2} = \frac{1}{s^2 + 4} + \frac{s}{s^2 + 4} \tag{3.17}$$

and

$$\bar{y} = -\frac{2}{s^2 + 4} \tag{3.18}$$

Taking inverse laplace transform of equation (3.17) we have

$$x = \frac{1}{2}\sin 2t + \cos 2t \tag{3.19}$$

Taking inverse laplace transform of equation (3.18) we have

$$y = -\sin 2t \tag{3.20}$$

Now from given question we have to verify that the value x and y will satisfy the equation

$$4x^2 + 4xy + 5y^2 = 4$$

Now putting the value of x and y from equation (3.19) and (3.20) in L.H.S. above equation we have

$$4[\tfrac{1}{2}\sin 2t + \cos 2t]^2 + 4[\tfrac{1}{2}\sin 2t + \cos 2t][-\sin 2t] + 5[-\sin 2t]^2$$

$$\implies \quad 4[\tfrac{1}{4}\sin^2 2t + \cos^2 2t + \sin 2t\cos 2t] - [2\sin^2 2t + 4\sin 2t\cos 2t] + 5\sin^2 2t$$

$$\implies \quad 4\sin^2 2t + 4\cos^2 2t = 4 = \text{R.H.S.}$$

Thus the particle moves along the curve $4x^2 + 4xy + 5y^2 = 4$.

Example 13 Using the laplace transforms, solve the initial value problem $y_1^{''} = y_1 + 3y_2$ and $y_2^{''} = 4y_1 - 4e^t$ with initial conditions $y_1(0) = 2,\ y_1^{'}(0) = 3,\ y_2(0) = 1,\ y_1^{'}(0) = 2.$

Sol. The given equation can be written as

$$y_1^{''} = y_1 + 3y_2 \tag{3.21}$$

and

$$y_2^{''} = 4y_1 - 4e^t \tag{3.22}$$

Taking laplace transform of above equations and given using initial conditions we have

$$(s^2 - 1)\bar{y}_1 - 3\bar{y}_2 = 2s + 3 \tag{3.23}$$

and

$$4\bar{y}_1 - s^2\bar{y}_2 = \frac{4}{s-1} - s - 2 \tag{3.24}$$

On solving equations (3.23) and (3.24) we get

$$\bar{y}_1 = \frac{1}{s-1} + \frac{1}{s-2} \tag{3.25}$$

and

$$\bar{y}_2 = \frac{1}{s-2} \tag{3.26}$$

Taking inverse laplace transforms of equations (3.25) and (3.26) we have

$$y_1 = e^t + e^{2t} \qquad \text{and} \qquad y_2 = e^{2t}.$$

3.2 Miscellaneous Exercise

1. Applying convoltion theorem, solve the following initial value problem $y^{''} + y = \sin 3t, \quad y(0) = 0, \ y^{'}(0) = 0.$
Ans. $y = \frac{1}{8}(3\sin t - \sin 3t).$
2. Apply laplace transform to solve the equation $\frac{d^2y}{dt^2} + y = t\cos 2t, \quad t > 0,$ given that $y = \frac{dy}{dt} = 0 \quad \text{for } t = 0.$
Ans. $-\frac{5}{9}\sin t + \frac{4}{9}\sin 2t - \frac{t}{3}\cos 2t.$
3. Using laplace transform, solve the following differential equation:

$$y^{''} + 2ty^{'} - y = t \quad \text{when} \quad y(0) = 0 \text{ and } y^{'}(0) = 1.$$

Ans. $y = t.$
4. A particle moves in a line so that its displacement x from a fixed point O at any time t, is given by

$$\frac{d^2x}{dt^2} + 4\frac{dx}{dt} + 5x = 80\sin 5t$$

Using laplace transform, find its displacement at any time t if initially particle is at rest at $x = 0$.
Ans. $2e^{-2t}(\cos t + 7\sin t) - 2(\cos 5t + \sin 5t).$
5. Solve the following differential equations by using laplace transform:

$$\frac{d^2y}{dx^2} + \frac{dy}{dx} - 2y = 1 - 2x, \qquad \text{given } y = 0, \ \frac{dy}{dx} = 4 \text{ at } x = 0.$$

Ans. $y = e^x - e^{-2x} + x.$
6. A resistance R in series with inductance L is connected with e.m.f. $E(t)$. The current i is given by

$$L\frac{di}{dt} + Ri = E \quad \text{where} \quad E(t) = \begin{cases} E, & 0 < t < a \\ 0, & t > a \end{cases}$$

If the switch is connected at $t = 0$ and disconnected at $t = a$, find the current i in terms of t.
Ans. $i = \frac{E}{R}e^{-\frac{R}{L}t}[e^{\frac{Ra}{L}} - 1]$.
7. Solve the simultaneous equations: $\frac{dx}{dt} - y = e^t$, and $\frac{dy}{dt} + x = \sin t$ given $x(0) = 1,\ y(0) = 0$.
Ans. $x = \frac{1}{2}[e^t + \cos t + 2\sin t - t\cos t]$ and $y = \frac{1}{2}[t\sin t - e^t + \cos t - \sin t]$.
8. Use laplace transform to solve $\frac{dx}{dt} + y = \sin t$, and $\frac{dy}{dt} + x = \cos t$ given that $x = 2,\ y = 0$ at $t = 0$.
Ans. $x = e^{-t} + e^t$ and $y = \sin t + e^{-t} - e^t$.
9. Solve the following simultaneous differential equations by laplace transform $\frac{dx}{dt} + 4\frac{dy}{dt} - y = 0,\ \ \frac{dx}{dt} + 2y = e^{-t}$ with conditions $x(0) = y(0) = 0$.
Ans. $x = \frac{1}{3} - \frac{5}{7}e^{-t} + \frac{8}{21}e^{3t/4}$ and $y = \frac{1}{7}(e^{-t} - e^{3t/4})$.
10. Using laplace transform, solve $(D-2)x - (D+1)y = 6e^{3t}$ and $(2D-3)x + (D-3)y = 6e^{3t}$ given that $x = 3, y = 0$ when $t = 0$.
Ans. $x = e^t + 2te^t + 2e^{3t}$ and $y = \sinh t + \cosh t - e^{-3t} - te^t$.
11. Solve the simultaneous equations $(D^2-3)x - 4y = 0$ and $x + (D^2+1)y = 0$ for $t > 0$, given that $x = y = \frac{dy}{dt} = 0$ and $\frac{dx}{dt} = 2$ at $t = 0$.
Ans. $x = 2t\cosh t,\ y = (1-t)\sinh t$.

Bibliography

[1] **Raisinghania, M. D.:** Integral Transform, S. Chand & Company Ltd., **(1995)**.

[2] **Dass, H. K. and Verma, Rama:** Introduction to Engineering Mathematics, Vol. II, S. Chand & Company Ltd., **(2015)**.

[3] **Das, P. S. and Vijaykumari, C.:** Engineering Mathematics, Pearson India Education Services Pvt. Ltd., **(2018)**.

[4] **Bali, N. P., Goyal, Manish and Gupta, Satinder Bal:** A Testbook of Engineering Mathematics, University Science Press, **(2022)**.

[5] **Grawal, B. S.:** Higher Engineering Mathematics, Khanna Publications, **(1965)**.

[6] **Spiegel:** Laplace Transforms, Schaum's outline series, McGraw Hill Publibations **(2005)**.

[7] **Schiff, J. L.:** The Laplace Transform, Springer, **(1999)**.

[8] **Gorain, G. C.:** The Laplace Transformations, Narosa Publications, **(2014)**.

[9] **Davies, B.:** Integral Transform and their Applications, Springer New York, **(2013)**.

www.ingramcontent.com/pod-product-compliance
Lightning Source LLC
LaVergne TN
LVHW070943160826
845679LV00022B/1894

* 9 7 9 8 8 9 7 4 4 7 0 7 7 *